Teachers and the Reform of Elementary Science: Stories of Conversation and Personal Process

A Volume in
Issues in Curriculum Theory, Policy, and Research

By: Heidi Bulmahn Barker
Series Editors: Ian Westbury and Margery D. Osborne

For my father

Teachers and the Reform of Elementary Science: Stories of Conversation and Personal Process

by
Heidi Bulmahn Barker
University of Colorado at Denver

Series Editors
Ian Westbury
Margery D. Osborne

INFORMATION AGE
PUBLISHING

80 Mason Street • Greenwich, Connecticut 06830 • www.infoagepub.com

Library of Congress Cataloging-in-Publication Data

Teachers and the reform of elementary science : stories of conversation
and personal process / edited by Heidi Bulmahn Barker.
    p. cm. — (Issues in curriculum theory, policy, and research)
Includes bibliographical references and index.
  ISBN 1-59311-103-7 (hardcover) — ISBN 1-59311-102-9 (pbk.)
  1. Science—Study and teaching (Elementary)—United States—Case
studies. 2. Science teachers—United States—Case studies. 3.
Curriculum change—United States—Case studies. I. Barker, Heidi
Bulmahn. II. Series.
  LB1585.3.T413 2004
  372.3'5'044—dc22

                                               2003024780

CONTENTS

Acknowledgments   vii

1. **INTRODUCTION**   **1**
   Introduction: One Curriculum, Two Classrooms   1
   My Own Background and Experience with Reform: 4
       A Lens for this Project
   Teacher Thinking: A Review of Some Related Literature   6
   School Change: Some Related Literature   9
   Thinking About Changes   10
   My Role and Research "Methods"   12
   Stories as Research: Using Narrative in Teacher Research   14

2. **THE RESEARCH CONTEXT: BALMORAL, REFORM,**   **27**
   AND STANDARDIZED TESTS
   Have We Learned the Things to Pass the Test?   27
   A Unique Community: The Research Site   29
   Conversations About Reform and Conversations   35
       About Standards: Creating Tension
   No Time for Wondering   48

3. **RELATIONSHIPS**   **51**
   Making Space for Reform/Change or Taking Space   51
       from Reform/Change
   Protecting a Collaborative Relationship   52
   Collaborating with Each Other   53
   Is What We're Doing Consistent with What We Believe?   56
   Collaborating Toward Change   59
   Process and Product in Teaching and Learning: 64
       Relationships with the Children and
       Relationships with the Curriculum
   Tensions of Teaching: Implicit and Explicit Science   65
   Concluding Notes   67

4. STRUCTURAL SUPPORTS   **71**
   A Story About "Stuff"   71
   Structural Supports   74
   Supporting Teachers: A Personal Process Amidst   85
      Group Change

5. COLLABORATION AND OWNERSHIP   **89**
   What is Collaboration?: Product and Process   89
   Collaborative Spaces: Lingering Questions   94
   Imposing a Curriculum   96
   Gail's Story: Ownership of the Planning and Teaching   101
   Sandy's Story: Already Owning the Ideas of Reform   103
   Liz's Story: Taking Ownership by Doing   104
   Women's Ways of Knowing: Teachers Finding Ownership   105

6. A ROOM OF ONE'S OWN: CONCRETE AND   **107**
    CONCEPTUAL SPACES
   Jennie's Story (Part 1): A Room of One's Own   107
   Teachers as Space Makers   109
   Alice's Story: Creating a Space of Her Own   109
   David's Story: Conversation for Making His Own   112
      Understanding
   Jennie's Story (Part 2): A Comfort Zone   115
   Questioning the Process   116
   Individual Spaces   117

7. NEGOTIATING A SPACE TO TEACH SCIENCE   **121**
   Individuality Within the Context of Community   122
   Imposed Changes and Teachers' Own Practice   126
   Change as a Process, Not a Location   127
   Laura's Story: A Process of Change   129
   Learning Communities and Personal Reform Experience   134

REFERENCES   **137**

INDEX   **141**

ACKNOWLEDGMENTS

This work was completed at the University of Illinois at Urbana-Champaign. I would like to thank Liora Bresler, Walter Feinberg, Susan E. Noffke, and Margery D. Osborne. I would particularly like to acknowledge the gentle guidance and support of Margery.

Marilyn Sinclair is also a mentor and sage. Thank you for your contributions and your continued enthusiasm for teaching and learning.

Thanks to Ian Westbury for guiding me throuh the process of putting this work into book format and navigating me through the publishing process.

Thanks to my family—my parents and husband. And to my two daughters, Grace and Elizabeth, who have grown with the project—their presence is certainly a part of this work.

Mostly, I must thank the teachers whose voices and experiences I have tried to document in the following pages. I appreciate the ways that you let me be a part of your teaching and learning experience—inviting me into your classrooms, your meetings, and your conversations.

CHAPTER 1

INTRODUCTION

INTRODUCTION:
ONE CURRICULUM, TWO CLASSROOMS

I sit down in the back of the third grade classroom in Balmoral,[1] Illinois while the teacher finishes giving his instructions. "Please make sure that you take this note home to your parents," he is saying. The teacher is referring to a sheet of paper he has prepared to remind the students and their parents of an upcoming vocabulary quiz. He hands me one of the papers and I read it to myself while the kids move their desks into groups of two to begin their science experiments:

> Dear Parents,
>
> Our science class will be having a quiz over these vocabulary words on Thursday, September 16. Each student has an envelope with words and matching definitions. If you have questions please call. Thank you for taking the time to work with your child.
>
> Mr. McDonald

Listed below the note to the parents are the vocabulary words that Mr. McDonald has assigned to go with the unit on rocks and minerals that the third grade class is studying:

1. fossils: plants, bones, or sea shells that got caught in layers of rock.
2. sediment: bits and pieces that have settled to the bottom of water.

Teachers and the Reform of Elementary Science, 1–26

3.   magma: melted underground rock.
4.   lava: magma that erupts through the surface of the earth
5.   igneous: rocks formed from magma.
6.   metamorphic: rocks that have been changed by underground pressure or heat.

The children have now begun their activities with the minerals that they are studying. The pairs of students are working through a series of tests on a set rocks. They have sheets of paper where they are recording their results. The tests are specific and include directions to cause the children to describe the rock in terms of color, size, hardness, shape, smell, translucency, and others. The students will use the information that they have gathered to classify their rocks and minerals. The students also read information about the rocks and minerals that will help them in making the classifying decisions.

In another third grade classroom, the teacher passes out a sheet of "describing words." The students will use these sheets as guides as they complete a chart about their rocks. She is using the scientific activities of observing and describing to prepare the students for the state writing test in which they may have to compose a descriptive paragraph. These students are also working in groups and are using magnifying lenses to look closely at the rocks and minerals. They will use the information they discover to classify rocks and minerals as well as the information they gathered by reading materials and books. The students as a class compiled the list of words together with their definitions from their combined inquiry and research:

Describing Words
1.   Feels: rough, bumpy, uneven, coarse, smooth, even, jagged, scaly, light (in weight), heavy, lumpy, sandy
2.   Looks: names of colors, shiny, glisteny, sparkly, clear, transparent, glossy, bright, fluorescent, dull, crystally, shimmering, holey, has vertical/horizontal lines
3.   Size: large, medium, small, tiny, little
4.   Smell: sulfur, rotten eggs, burnt match, smoky, salty, muddy, dirt, sandy
5.   Shape: oval, round-shapes, triangle, rectangle, square, circular

The kids began to write sentences which described the rocks. "My rock is reddish-pink in color. It has some sparkly parts and vertical lines. It feels uneven and is a rectangle. It doesn't have any smell. Cody brought it from her trip to Colorado." The students also drew a picture of the rock to accompany their prose.

In both classrooms the students worked on the science process skills of classifying, describing, and experimenting. The goals of the lessons were similar, but the ways that the teachers went about setting up the learning was approached in different ways—ways that reflect not only their own personal beliefs about the ways that teaching and learning take place, but also their sense of the influence of their state, their community, their building, their students, and their peers. The way the lessons were implemented in the classroom was a reflection of the teacher. A teacher's classroom is his or her own space. It is a space that is occupied not only physically but also mentally while engaging in the creative act of teaching and making decisions about the whats and the hows of the ways that the curriculum will be enacted. Many factors influence these decisions (colleagues, state, national, and local standards, administration, community, etc.), but it is the different ways that every teacher creates his or her own physical and conceptual space for teaching that is interesting to me. I assert: *teachers create their own spaces for making changes in pedagogy and curriculum and they do this as a complex negotiation of external demands and their own values and interpretations.*

Both of these classrooms were part of a project where the teachers in Balmoral, Illinois were working to move from a textbook-based science curriculum to an inquiry, activity-based curriculum. The work of this reform effort took place over a two-year period. During this time the teachers attempted to find the ways that the new curriculum worked in their classrooms. They tried the science out on their own, with their students, and with each other—both actively and through conversations. Implementing the new science curriculum fit with many teachers' philosophies about how science should be taught and for others it was a big change. Negotiation and questioning of the pedagogy and the curriculum in their own classrooms became a part of the journey for all of the teachers. Throughout this book, I will explore the negotiation of the ways that teachers are involved in the process of changing curriculum and pedagogies and also the realities of implementing those changes in the classroom. How do teachers negotiate their place within changes in pedagogy and curriculum and how is this negotiation enacted in the space of a teacher's own classroom?

That is the question that I will explore by telling stories about the process of change and the ways that teachers were involved with curricular and pedagogical reform efforts imposed in their particular school district. This chapter sets up perspectives (my background and interests, my role in this project, and my research methods) that I bring to this project. In Chapter 2 I will describe the research site, this project, science reform efforts, standardized, and achievement tests in an attempt to show how these shape the context of this project. Chapter 3 tells stories of the ways that relationships (relationships between teachers, between teachers and the curriculum, and between teachers and children) play a role in the way that reforms are enacted in classrooms. Chapter 4 explores the manner in which structural supports can help individual teachers work through their doubts, their excitement, and their own ideas related to reform efforts. Chapter 5 explores issues of ownership. I will give examples of teachers who felt a part of the project and those who did not. I will question what it means to collaborate, and more specifically how collaborative relationships between researchers and teachers effect reform efforts. Chapter 6 argues that teachers work in their own conceptual and concrete spaces and that reform efforts need to allow teachers to find the space where they can work to make changes in their teaching and learning. In Chapter 7, I will attempt to bring these ideas together asking more questions about how change can occur in schools. I will argue that change is a process and ultimately a personal process that takes place within a context of these other issues (relationships, community, society, school structures).

MY OWN BACKGROUND AND EXPERIENCE WITH REFORM: A LENS FOR THIS PROJECT

After a grade-level meeting at Franklin Science Center in Champaign where teachers were brainstorming with each other, planning science topics, looking at science materials and supplies, and comparing their science teaching experiences, Marilyn Sinclair, who was leading the meeting, and I rode together to eat lunch. In the car we began to talk about an experience that both of us shared. These experiences took place two decades apart (Marilyn has been involved in education for over 30 years and I about 10) and in different states, but were so similar that we wished we could reproduce them in the Balmoral schools. Each of us had taught one year in a magnet school that was newly opened with hand-picked faculty hired to facilitate active learning and curriculum building. We both spoke about the energy that resonated from that experience, how exciting it was to be a part of teaching that seemed exciting and positive, and where the faculty seemed to thrive from knowing that they had a say in how the teaching and the curriculum were formed. We talked about the collegiality between teachers, the sharing of ideas, and the way that planning and brainstorming ideas together created that energy that seemed to be transmitted from teacher to teacher and from teacher to student.

My experiences as a classroom teacher have given me the context for my interest in teacher relationships. As a classroom teacher, I felt most successful when I was able to collaborate with other teachers. The process of planning and creating curriculum together, it seemed, gave us a special relationship with the materials and activities. The very act of creating curriculum, whether the impetus for the topics was derived through established standards, emanated from the students, or was personally chosen by us, established a special relationship to the materials and activities resulting from that creative process. We not only developed curriculum, but also an interest and excitement for the material, an ownership of the activities, and a personal satisfaction that made the curriculum our own. This direct involvement also seemed to make it easier to encourage our students to find and create their own relationship with the content. It seemed easier to help children find their own excitement for the learning process when we were directly involved in the process ourselves. Being involved in the process of creating, designing, and implementing new curriculum and pedagogy gave me as a teacher an experience that somewhat paralleled the experience of the students in my class; I was experimenting, discussing, learning, making decisions and connections to my own previous knowledge, et cetera. I wanted to have this control over the pedagogy and curriculum and was also given the opportunity by my administration, my community, and supported by colleagues. Because of this personal experience, I became interested in exploring how teachers negotiate their role in school reform. I began to wonder in what ways do they create changes in curriculum and pedagogy and what inspires some to do so and others to seem satisfied with the way things are?

I give this background to give a sense of the lenses with which I had coming into the project, what sorts of things might bias my project, and to give a sense of what is important to me in teaching and learning. I very much value creativity and relationships. I am also interested in the teacher's role in school reform. Taking my interests into account, I realize that the scope of my research has limitations. I acknowledge that the teacher's impact on the learning that takes place in his or her classroom is only one part of the learning process—an important part, but only one part of an equation which includes many variables. I am not looking at the ways that kids perceive the curriculum, evaluation of the curriculum, and so forth, I am looking at the personal process of educational change that manifests itself in the form of pedagogical and curricular decisions that happen every day in every teacher's classroom. I will explore the ways that individual teachers negotiate between their own personal values for teaching and learning (as enacted in their individual classrooms) and external factors (such as their community, their colleagues, the state standards) and their personal interpretations of these external factors.

My own experiences as a teacher and my experiences in working with the teachers at Balmoral has led me to formulate the question that this book is based on: How do teachers negotiate their place within changes in pedagogy and curriculum? How will changing (1) the ways that science is taught and learned, and (2) the content of the science that is taught and learned affect the state tests? This question came up over and over as I talked to teachers who began to try the curriculum in their classrooms. They seemed to like the enthusiasm of the children for learning science and the involvement of the kids in their projects and learning, but that question lurked in the back of their minds. As the teachers were given more control in the decisions they made about the direction their curriculum and teaching would go, they began to wonder if these decisions and directions were the "right" ones. Do I believe in this? Is this what the state, the district, my students, the community, and what my administration expects and wants from learning? The journey of that process (the questioning and the decision making) is important.

Teachers negotiate between their own personal values for teaching and learning (as enacted in their individual classrooms) and external factors (such as their community, their colleagues, the state standards) and their personal interpretations of these external factors. Teachers find what works best for them or at least what they can work with in their classrooms after taking in the ideas and expectations of the "others" (external factors) and find ways that these changes fit with their own ideas. This is a complex process that manifests itself in the form of pedagogical and curricular decisions that happen every day in every teacher's classroom. In the next section, I explore literature related to the decisions that teachers make about pedagogy and curriculum.

TEACHER THINKING:
A REVIEW OF SOME RELATED LITERATURE

Elbaz (1983) studied what she calls "the practical knowledge" of a teacher. She defines teacher knowledge as:

> In program planning and instruction, we see teachers choosing among alternative materials, deciding how to adapt programs to the needs of particular classes, combining materials to make up new curriculum packages, writing units and complete programs, and putting these into use in the classroom.... [T]he teacher exhibits wide-ranging knowledge which grows as experience increases. This knowledge encompasses firsthand experiences of students' learning styles' interests, needs, strengths and difficulties, and a repertoire of instructional techniques and classroom management skills. The teacher knows the social structure of the school and what it requires, of teacher and student, for survival and success; she knows the community of which the school is a part, and has a sense of what it will and will not accept. This experiential knowledge is informed by the teacher's theoretical knowledge of subject matter, and of areas such as child development, learning and social theory. All of these kinds of knowledge, as integrated by the indi-

vidual teacher in terms of personal values and beliefs and as oriented to her practical situation, ... [are] "practical knowledge." (p. 5)

Craig (1995) defines teacher thinking as she describes the two different worlds that a teacher lives in. These two worlds are the classroom where teachers "co-construct meaning" with students and "the abstract world where [teachers] meet all the other aspects of the educational enterprise such as the philosophies, the techniques, the materials, and the expectations that [she] will enact certain educational practices" (p. 16). She goes on to complete her definition of knowledge as a teacher as a combination of these two places, neither self-contained, and calls this knowledge "professional knowledge landscape." This term is taken from Clandinin and Connelly (1995),

> A landscape metaphor is particularly suited to our purpose. It allows us to talk about space, place, and time ... it has a sense of expansiveness and the possibility of being filled with diverse people, things, and events in different relationships. (p. 4)

This metaphor and the definitions that incorporate the many entities that impact teacher decision making are well suited to the description of the ways that the teachers in Balmoral described their questions, concerns and experiences with the science reforms. "[T]eachers do not neutrally implement theories and programs; they develop programs of study for their classrooms by adaptation, translation, and modification of given programs and research findings" (Connelly & Elbaz, 1980, p. 107).

What the teacher chooses to do with the materials is the main force in whether a child will understand the concepts and ideas. The potential of the curriculum program is embodied in the choices that a teacher makes. (Connelly & Clandinin, 1988, p. 149). Ben-Peretz explores this concept and names it "curriculum potential." Ben-Peretz and Kremer (1979) show that even when efforts are made to train teachers to implement curriculum materials, the success of the implementation still depends on the teachers' interpretations of the materials. Taking this idea further, Ball and Cohen (1996) examine the idea of curriculum materials and their impact on educational reform. They argue that developers fail to take into account the differences in the ways that teachers utilize and implement the developers ideas, similar to the theory of "curriculum potential" (Ben-Peretz, 1990). Ben-Peretz argues that although teachers do rely on the activities included in texts, each teacher approaches the material in a different manner and that is part of the creative planning process. "[I]ndividual teachers shape the curriculum in fundamental ways.... [Their] understanding of the material, their beliefs about what is important, and their ideas about students and the teacher's role all strongly shape their practice" (Ball & Cohen, 1996, p. 6).

Barham (1996) examines the concept of imposed curriculum and teacher creativity in her study. How do teachers adapt and implement imposed curriculum? This study focused on the role of teachers in adapting an imposed national curriculum in the United Kingdom. The curriculum studied had a strong central control. She compares this to the current mode of thinking in the United States—the imposition of standards in many states and the debate over national testing. Despite the government's attempts to "change what we want our children to learn to how do we control what our children learn" (p. 31) by mandating curriculum reform to be imposed on teachers, curriculum cannot be made "teacher-proof." Instead, as Barham notes, teachers took control of the curriculum and intertwined it with the curriculum they were already creating and using in their classrooms. With the knowledge of what works and what does not is the understanding that "teachers have, in fact, maintained observable power over the process of change—in the day-to-day translation of centrally imposed texts into the action of the classroom" (p. 34). Teachers utilize their knowledge to create the curriculum that fits in their classroom, despite constraints placed on them. Olson (1980) also found that as teachers implemented a new science program, they adapted the new project elements and translated them into a workable teaching system. The teachers used methods similar to those already well known (p. 6).

Ben-Peretz and Tamir (1981) also studied the impact of imposed curriculum. They researched teachers' views and concerns in relation to the centrally produced Israeli school curriculum. The author attempted to answer two questions: (a) What questions do teachers have about curriculum materials, and (b) How do teachers see themselves in their role as curriculum implementers? The conclusions show that teachers are concerned most with "subject matter" aspects of the curriculum and that they really do not see themselves as having a role in the implementation process. These results seem to show that if a curriculum is imposed from an outside source, teachers do not take accountability or ownership for the implementation of the curriculum. This seems to contradict the findings of other studies which show that teachers make an "imposed curriculum" their own by adapting it to their students' needs, their content needs, and their activity ideas.

Teachers do make choices about how to implement materials, but it is not a choice that is made in isolation. The choices are made through an examination of their own values and beliefs, the values and beliefs of the community, the students, and the governing bodies of their position. The choices are also based on children's needs, the composition of the class, and the time allotted for teaching. In many cases the choices are based on a number of factors, including the teacher's prior experience and what she or he believes about teaching and learning. These individual choices impact the ways that reform is manifested in classrooms. The teachers in Balmoral began to negotiate these factors as they began to change the district science curriculum.

SCHOOL CHANGE: SOME RELATED LITERATURE

Much of what has been written about school change and reform efforts has been directed toward administrative and policy-making agendas. I want to acknowledge this literature as it does include the teacher in making changes and decisions in schools, but it does so from a different angle that what I am examining here. "Acknowledging the teacher's purpose and understanding and valuing the teacher as a person ... should therefore be vital elements underpinning any strategy of staff development and school improvement" (Fullan & Hargreaves, 1996, p. 31). "Teachers will implement curriculum successfully if they have been involved in its development and can adapt it to their specific classroom and school situation" (Glickman, 1990, p. 360). In that particular body of literature, the focus has been on what structures and supports can be put into place to promote and facilitate change and to reach the standards, benchmarks, and goals of reform, listing things like understanding the culture of the school, promoting teachers' professional growth, goal-setting, promote collaboration and teamwork, give teachers choices, facilitate changes, supportive school climates, team teaching and team-oriented staff development (Schmoker, 1996; Sergiovanni & Starratt, 1993; Fullan & Hargreaves, 1996). Fullan and Hargreaves (1996, p. 64) give teachers a specific list of the changes that they can make themselves to promote school reform, individual responsibility, and collaborative culture. This list called "Guidelines for Teachers" includes ideas such as:

1. Locate, listen to, and articulate your inner voice.
2. Practice reflection in action, on action, and about action.
3. Develop a risk-taking mentality.
4. Trust processes as well as people.
5. Appreciate the total person in working with others.
6. Commit to working with colleagues.
7. Seek variety and avoid Balkanization.
8. Redefine your role to extend beyond the classroom.
9. Balance work and life.

10. Push and support principals and other administrators to develop interactive professionalism.
11. Commit to continuous improvement and perpetual learning.
12. Monitor and strengthen the connection between your development and students' development.

The ideas presented in these lists are ones that can certainly contribute to promoting school reform, but there has been a limited focus on using this type of list, or specific actions that teachers and administrators can do to create a school where change can happen. Sarason (1996) discusses the problems of school change at length in his book *Revisiting "The Culture of the School and the Problem of Change."* Although Sarason discusses power issues related to teachers throughout the book—the need for teachers to be seen as professionals and for teachers to be a part of reform efforts— he concludes:

> No complicated, traditional social institution can be changed only from within. There has to be some support for change from within, but there also has to be strong external, powerful pressures for change, powerful in terms of numbers, influence, and legislative legal policymaking responsibilities. Absent those external pressures, the institution will continue to confirm the adage I stated repetitively in the book: the more things change, the more they stay the same. (p. 338)

Change, or reform, is described here through an institutional view. Individuals involved in the process of change are described and analyzed in their role as part of the system and as part of systematic change. The personal process of change is not the focus of his analysis. That personal process—the negotiations, the choices, the decisions, and the actions of that process—are the focus of my study, a focus that is an important aspect of reform efforts.

Although reform efforts need to be organized and structured and teachers and other involved do need to take responsibility and action, I would argue that change is a very personal process and no matter how the work of reform is organized and structured, teachers will construct their own "ways of knowing" the new curriculum and pedagogy. They will ultimately make choices that will determine how the change enacts itself in their classrooms.

THINKING ABOUT CHANGES

Nineteen ninety-seven was the year for science textbooks to be selected in the Balmoral elementary buildings. One of the teachers had gone to a curriculum development workshop and science camp with an educational consultant and former science coordinator for a school district, Marilyn Sinclair. That became the impetus to apply for an Illinois State Board of Education (ISBE) Science Literacy Grant. The teachers on a district-level science curriculum committee with representatives from each grade level decided to make a commitment to moving away from a set of textbooks in each classroom to a process-oriented approach to teaching and learning science. The grant was written to support the teachers in this commitment. Part of the school improvement plan was also written in conjunction to this commitment. "The district will continue to develop an inquiry-based approach to science instruction through a grant from the ISBE" (Illinois School Report Card, 1998).

The grant was written as a 2-year proposal and was a cooperative effort between the school district and the University of Illinois at Urbana-Champaign. Through this collaboration, the school district would gain:

> ongoing consultation and guidance in science curriculum design to meet state and national standards and the provision of graduate-level classes designed specifically for the Balmoral teachers and their needs in science teaching, including: (1) enhanced knowledge of science concepts and principles, and (2) instruction and experience in inquiry methods of teaching. (from ISBE Grant abstract, 1999, p. 4)

The graduate course was taught in the summer in conjunction with a summer science camp for elementary students in the district. Additional staff development, planning meetings, and support continued throughout the school year with a cooperative effort between the teachers, the administrators, and the university consultant and graduate student.

Written after initial meetings that included teachers on the science curriculum committee,[2] the curriculum coordinator for the district (who is also a grade school principal), a university professor (Margery Osborne), and the science consultant (Marilyn Sinclair),[3] the teachers made clear that they needed support "in their need for increased knowledge in the content of the sciences appropriate for elementary classrooms, and of the pedagogical skills for teaching an inquiry-based science program" (ISBE Grant, 1999, p. 4). The grant funded staff development designed to create experiences in which teachers learned how to teach science to children through inquiry methods by participating in a guided inquiry into teaching (Easley, 1990). Easley promotes the idea that teachers learning how to guide students in their study of science, promoting science reasoning processes (prediction, observation, explanation, evaluating evidence, making analogies, and devising other experiments), and fostering communication skills (speaking, listening, working in groups) will help to break down the authoritarian, content-driven science that many elementary teachers are more comfortable implementing in their classrooms (p. 87). To do this, teachers need to experience these methods themselves. The teachers try out the teaching methods, ask questions, discuss their observations and experiences, and look for answers. Time for conversations between teachers, between teachers and university personnel, and between administrators, teachers, and university personnel was integral to this process and was supported by the grant through providing substitutes, planning time, and in-service. The teachers tried out the methods not only during the summer science camp, where reflection on teaching and learning also occurred, but also in their classrooms during a two-year pilot period. During this pilot period the teachers taught the units they had chosen and developed, discussed with one another their experiences with the teaching and learning, and modified the unit for future teaching.[4] The ideas and questions of teachers were specifically incorporated in the process of change and were used in the process of implementing the new curriculum.

MY ROLE AND RESEARCH METHODS

I participated in the project through the two-year grant cycle. This means that I was able to work with the teachers throughout two full school years and during two summer science camp sessions. I made attempts to build relationships with the teachers and administrators with whom I was working. I was present in all three elementary buildings where the science curriculum had been implemented and let the teachers know that I was there to support their efforts, not to evaluate their performance as teachers. As stated earlier, I had multiple roles as a participant in the reform efforts. Foremost, I tried to support the teachers' efforts. I visited classrooms (as another set of hands, as a coteacher, as a participant in the lesson), I participated in planning sessions and meetings (both informal and formal), and I listened to the teachers and tried to act on their needs. I also taught an elementary class during the summer science camp and assisted with the teacher course.

When I visited classrooms, I let the teachers tell me how they wanted me to be a part of the lesson—as an observer, a helper, a coteacher, and so forth. They were not visited unless we had set appointments up beforehand; there were no surprises in my presence. The teachers were aware that I was working on a research project about teachers' involvement in school reform and seemed to be very open and candid in their conversations with me. They were aware that I was taping and taking notes about what we said. At times they asked that comments be "off the record" and I honored these requests readily.

In trying to understand the teachers and their efforts in the reform efforts, information was collected through a variety of sources and I think give a very rich and layered understanding of the change process in this school district's science program, including: classroom visits, planning meetings (both formal and informal), e-mail correspondence, interviews (both scheduled and spontaneous conversations), informal lunches and visits in the teacher's lounge, involvement in the summer science camp as a teacher, researcher, and facilitator, reading teacher journals from the summer science course, involvement in grade level planning meetings, and involvement in district science committee meetings. I used a tape recorder and took both reflective and descriptive notes during my involvement in the reform efforts. I worked with the teachers over the two-year period documenting their experiences, thoughts, questions, feelings, ideas and concerns about the reform initiatives in their science curriculum, and stories of teaching and learning. The documented experiences were analyzed and the information was marked, coded, and grouped into increasingly larger themes, ensuring that all pieces of information were accounted for and included.

Of course, although I have tried my best to bring objectivity to the presentation of my "data," I bring to this study my own perspective (see Lincoln & Guba, 1985). I have tried to give voice to the teachers involved in this project, but the perspective and the telling of these stories is my own. I spent much time discussing the ideas presented with teachers, with Marilyn and with Margery, who were all involved with the project to try to show an accurate and fair picture of the process of change in the Balmoral School District. A qualitative study like this is not meant to show a universal conclusive finding that can be implemented in every school to fix the problems of science education reform, but a study like this can show a picture of what happened in a particular school district, in particular classrooms, and with particular teachers. This unique perspective cannot create generalities (Stake, 1995), but can show particulars that create thought provoking ideas which may be relevant to other unique and particular school settings. In this qualitative study there is a search to understand this particular process of pedagogical and curricular change—by giving a description and my own analysis (see Eisner, 1991; Wolcott, 1994), I hope that the reader will come to an understanding of what happened in the portrait of this process provided.

By choosing particular stories to share in my writing, I have left out hundreds more. By choosing specific teachers to work with, I made decisions not to work as closely with others. Some teachers expressed an interest in working with me, some teachers had interesting stories to tell, and some teachers were a part of the grant project from the very beginning and thus I formed a relationship with them over time. In the end, I had worked with all elementary science teachers in the district and have tried to include aspects of their voices in this book. These choices ultimately have shaped the perspective and understandings that I have had on the project. The stories that I have included are excerpts from conversations and experiences that I participated in and observed throughout the two-year project. I believe that they give a representation of what happened and show most clearly the themes that became increasingly apparent as I worked through my "data." The stories that I use to show the findings of this study will hopefully offer insights into the experiences of teachers in times of curricular and pedagogical reform, and the ways that educational change impacts them as individuals in their own classroom practice.

STORIES AS RESEARCH:
USING NARRATIVE IN TEACHER RESEARCH

"All my life I've felt that there was something magical about people who could get into other people's minds and skin, who could take people like me out of ourselves and then take us back to ourselves."

—Lamott (1994, p. xxvii)

"Come and look at our *SOIL*. We don't call it dirt, you know." Excitement about the science project was evident in Jan's[5] voice. The teacher beckoned me from the hallway into her classroom. It was after school and the room was empty of children, but their presence in the room could still be felt. Notes from discussion were left on the board, art work was posted on the walls, and materials from the science activity were on the back table. "Now, tell me what you think. Are the worms getting enough air? Do you think the soil is too moist?" I looked in the covered aquarium holding each child's ziplock bag full of soil, plants, worms, and whatever other organisms might exist in the backyard soil the class was working with.

The second graders had just begun a science unit where they would learn about the properties of soil by doing—by inquiring about the soil, by observing with their senses, by performing experiments to find answers to questions, and by recording and reporting their observations. "The kids are really excited about their bags. Because the towel covers the aquarium to keep it dark like it is underground, the anticipation is almost too much! We open them in a few weeks. I really want the worms to be alive ... here look at their recordings." The teacher shows me one of her student's notebooks. Inside are drawings of his bag of soil. The student had drawn and labeled parts of his soil: "clump, lettuce, grass, red worm, soil, twig, burrow." The student had predicted that in five weeks he would find "soil, decomposing, and burrows." The soil in the ziplock bags is part of an experiment in making compost.

"Already, they are looking more closely at things. Look at these drawings of the worms. Look at the second drawing." She shows me two observational drawings. The second one titled "I Took a Closer Look" definitely shows a more observant "look." The child has labeled parts of the worm, drawn the segments, and shown in detail the shape of the curving worm.

This teacher is very excited about the projects she has implemented in her classroom and is eager to share her story with me. Jan showed me what she was doing in her classroom, showed her student's work to me, and described her teaching experience. How can stories like Jan's contribute to our knowledge about teaching? Do they have a place in teacher research? What do personal stories about curricular and pedagogical reform in classrooms contribute to conversations about school change?

Community Conversations

Collaborative conversation (Hollingsworth, 1994) as a method of inquiry may challenge the traditional ideas of research. How can simply talking together about concerns of practice be a method of research and how can talking together as a means of support contribute to the knowledge of both the teacher and the researcher? To me, this seems a very logical, practical, and realistic way of creating spaces for change. Conversation allows for a supportive structure and a format for gaining understanding. The playing field is leveled as the teachers become experts by talking about their practice, and the power of the researcher is taken away as he or she is not the expert, but a part of the conversation. The relationships formed through the conversations create a different context for talking that is not a "dialogue—similar to the conversation in a play or novel, which appears to have two or more voices, but which actually comes from one author's perspective"; it is more than "simply a discussion of prearranged topics and readings through a formal discourse structure" (Hollingsworth, 1994, p. 8). It is a collaborative and sustained conversation, an exchange and reformulation of ideas, intimate talk, and reconstructive questions. Throughout the conversation, common stories about learning to teach are understood. The "vague, almost subconscious questioning and tentative knowing about teaching school [is] thus elevated, voiced, and connected" (Hollingsworth, 1994, p. 8). The conversations that teachers share specifically about their teaching experiences give those experiences meaning for the teller and for the listener. The teller is an expert and the teaching experience is important enough to take time to listen and learn from the story. Dewey's (1916/1944) ideas about community and communication elaborate on the ways that conversation can enhance understanding:

> To be a recipiant of a communication is to have an enlarged and changed experience. One shares in what another has thought and felt and in so far, meagerly or amply, has his own attitude modified. Nor is the one who communicates left unaffected... The experience has to be formulated in order to be communicated. To formulate requires getting outside of it, seeing it as another would see it, considering what points of contact it has with the life of another so that it may be got into such a form that he can appreciate its meaning. (Dewey, 1916/1944, pp. 5-6)

When teachers talked about their experiences with the new science curriculum, reflected on their practices, and planned for future teaching, the teachers articulated their own understanding of the process. This articulation began to validate and connect their experiences to the ways that they view science teaching and learning.

Collaborative conversations were enacted in various forms as teachers began to implement the inquiry-based science curriculum. They took place between teachers of the same grade, between teachers across grade levels, between teachers and administrators, and between teachers and myself. As I visited classrooms, attended planning meetings, and participated in the summer science camp, we discussed stories of teaching in the context of exchanging ideas, questioning ideas, and how teaching and/or learning experiences were connected to one another. These conversations became my research "data." As teachers formed a closer relationship with the material and with each other, the conversation continued and contributed to reformulating their ideas and questions about their science teaching. The ideas and questions about their science teaching were what they began to explore more closely in the space of their own classrooms.

Why Narrative?

"Although a life is not a narrative, people make sense of their lives and the lives of others through narrative constructions" (Richardson, 1990, p. 65). "The main claim for the use of narrative in educational research is that humans are storytelling organisms who, individually and socially, lead storied lives. The study of narrative, therefore, is the study of the ways humans experience the world.... [T]eachers and learners are story-tellers and characters in their own and other's stories" (Connelly & Clandinin, 1990, p. 2). "[Narrative] is the closest to the human experience and hence the least falsifying of that experience, and it rejuvenates the sociological imagination in the service of liberatory civic discourses and transformative social projects" (Richardson, 1990, p. 65). Researchers give people a place to tell their stories—a place that may help in bringing about change, in exchanging ideas, and in understanding each other. "[P]eople by nature lead storied lives and tell stories of those lives, whereas narrative researchers describe such lives, collect and tell stories of them, and write narratives of experience"(Connelly & Clandinin, 1990, p. 2). By telling stories of classroom experiences, both the teacher and the researcher can attempt to make meaning of the complexities of teaching and learning.

Narrative inquiry can provide an agenda for both the researcher and the teacher. It is a way to connect theory and practice through collaborative stories. The practitioner and the researcher create a relationship in which they can "productively relate to each other" (Connelly & Clandinin, 1990, p. 12). As the researcher works to understand the teacher's narrative, the researcher becomes a part of the story and crafts a narrative that Clandinin and Connelly have named a collective story.

> Scribes we were not; story tellers and story livers we were. And in our own story telling, the stories of our participants merged with our own to create new stories, ones that we have labeled collective stories ... a collaborative document, a mutually constructed story created out of the lives of both researcher and participant. (p. 12)

Narrative inquiry can also give a powerful sense of the whole. Through interviews, fieldnotes, observation, and collaborative discussions (Clandinin & Connelly, 1994) the researcher can put together parts of the story that build a big picture to understanding teaching and learning. Grumet (1987) talks about the way that multiple narratives contribute to our understanding of the world.

> Multiple narratives make it possible for us to go beyond, and around the text, to research it without accusing it of false consciousness, on one hand, or succumbing to its rationale on the other. It permits [us] to construct a question about [the work] we will do together.... Others ... will read his texts differently, and with them he will develop different questions that he will bring to his work. Multiple texts and multiple interpreters bring the presentation of personal knowledge out of the whispered confidences of the analytic dyad ... into a community of people who share a world. (Grumet, 1987, p. 327)

Every reader will bring a different lens to the reading, interacting with the story, and building an understanding of the person, events, or experience described.

Bateson (1989) utilizes multiple narratives to write about women's experience and the ways that women form the experience of their lives. She utilizes the stories of four women along with her own narrative in weaving together the experiences that many women share as they "compose" their own life stories. Her metaphor of a quilt describes this composition:

> At the same time, you cannot put together a life willy-nilly from odds and ends. Even in a crazy quilt, the various pieces, wherever they come from, have to be trimmed and shaped and arranged how they fit together, then firmly sewn to last through time and keep out the cold. Most quilts are more ambitious: they involve the imposition of a new pattern. But even crazy quilts are sewn against a backing; the basic sense of continuity allows improvisation. Composing a life involves an openness to possibilities and the capacity to put them together in a way that is structurally sound. (p. 63)

Although Bateson is talking about putting a life together here, the words could very easily be used to describe the way that she has formed her narrative. The pieces of the story are not put together "willy-nilly." They are crafted in a way that lets the reader see the whole picture of her "research topic."

The story of the second grade teacher and her excitement about the science activities is only a partial narrative. It only begins to show the reader the needs of a teacher to share her successful teaching experiences, to ask for an outside opinion to validate her feelings, and to help the researcher understand the complexities of her implementation of a new curriculum. As individual stories of teaching and learning unfold, the personal processes of change begins to unfold. Because they are personal stories the teachers tell about the differing ways that they are dealing with change, narratives of this story differ from the way that school change issues are often represented. It is not new to state that teachers are an important aspect of school reform (see Evans, 1996; Fullan & Hargreaves, 1996; Lieberman, 1995; Schwille et al., 1983; Spillane, 1999; Wagner, 1994) but the vision is often a list (as I discussed earlier) of what structures can be put into place—a recipe type list that will help to build a school culture that creates, sustains, and motivates good teachers throughout their careers (Fullan & Hargreaves, 1996, p. 63). The lists, although including important aspects of structural supports, are not concerned with the personal and individual aspects and efforts of teachers' experiences with the reform efforts. The individual stories further our understanding that change is a complex and individual process.

My Space as a Researcher: What is My Role?

If one of the goals of narrative is to craft the big picture, to put the pieces of the story together in such a way that others can relate to and understand the experiences of the teachers and their work, how does the researcher do this? I have found myself in several roles as I try to put together a "quilt" of understanding as I work on this project.

As teachers worked to move away from a text-oriented science program to an inquiry, process-based approach that includes hands on activities, integration of other subject areas, and in-depth study of topics, my role has been to support the classroom teachers in the design and implementation process. Support as enacted and defined has been a dual process, a collaborative activity, balancing my own needs as a researcher and the needs of the teachers. My role was different at the end of the project than it was at the very beginning and it changed depending on the teacher(s) with which I was working.

For some teachers, I came to this project as the university expert. This was their preconceived notion of the way that they should interact with someone from the university. Until our relationships grew and trust was formed, they perceived me as someone there to judge their teaching, not as a learner. Once they saw me in their classrooms, interacting with students, and discussing with them the experience of teaching did my role change. They continued to ask me questions that an expert should know: How warm should the soil be kept through the winter? Will a regular fluorescent light bulb or a grow lamp work better for our plant experiments? What is cross-fertilization? But, my role expanded as I became a part of the experience of implementing the new curriculum. I have named these roles[6]: (1) researcher as learner, (2) researcher as listener, (3) researcher as validator, and (4) researcher as artist.

Researcher as Learner

As stated earlier, the way that support has been defined and enacted has changed and continued to change as I worked with the teachers in a collaborative manner. I tried to let both of our needs create the enactment and definition. As the role changed in my eyes, it also may have changed in the teacher's eyes. Hollingsworth (1994) suggests that you show yourself as a learner by making public your own struggle with learning. The teachers must understand that I was not there to be the expert but to learn along with them.[7] Part of my learning was always to try to make an understanding for myself the process the teachers were going through, and that I, in a more limited sense, am going through with them. The relationship needed to be constructed so that each individual could contribute to the understanding and the learning. We could all be experts.

The conversational approach to learning to teach included environmental aspects that supported the political and philosophical nature of our work.... [T]he social context of our dinner meetings allowed all of us to take the floor as "experts" in special areas of interest and teaching. The safety of our continuing relationship provided many occasions for raising questions, for sharing the passion and frustration of what we were learning in our own voices, and for confronting our anger about our silence and lack of appropriate support in other settings. (Hollingsworth, 1994, p. 5)

I also tried to set up situations where conversations could take place: meetings between teachers after school, informal in-services, scheduled planning sessions. The frequent discussions were held with collegial groups of teachers for the purpose of reflection on their own growth in understanding and examination of perceived effects of the curriculum on student learning and attitudes toward science. These conversations provided a nonthreatening opportunity for teachers and administrators and researchers to reach common understandings and trust in the learning climate of the classroom, including the methods of teaching, the effectiveness of the curricular materials, and the variety of assessment methods used to evaluate student learning. Teachers met as they piloted science units to share progress and to discuss problems, solutions, and ideas for integrating the topics with other disciplines. Teachers also met at the completion of units to reflect on their teaching practices. In addition to reflecting on their own practices, teachers communicated their experiences to teachers who had not yet piloted the units. This exchange of questions and ideas facilitated reflection and planning. This collegial sharing is an integral part of program development and classroom implementation.

A Reflection on Planting: Sharing Ideas through Conversation

Two sixth grade teachers shared their experience with a unit titled "Experiments with Plants" with another sixth grade teacher who was about to begin the unit in her classroom. I set up the meeting, but was not the expert—the teachers who had completed the unit were the experts. I was a learner, listening to what the teachers had to say about their experience. We sat at student desks in Mary's room. Each of us had our unit outline and the supplies for the unit were spread on the floor around us. It was after school and the teachers were tired, but I could tell that Mary and Rob were proud to share their experiences and Ramona was eager to hear what they had to say.

> **Mary:** I think it really went well. Our main problem was the
> waiting while the plants grew. We added in a couple of

projects—a "bee poster" and a plant journal. I made copies of what we did for you.

Ramona: Where did the kids get the information to complete these? (She looks at the project pages.)

Mary: I just went up town and had the librarian pull all the books on bees.

Rob: The books were mostly picture books, but the kids really liked getting the bee facts and looking at the pictures. Also that video on pollination was really good.

Mary: We found out that the stakes are very important and those little plastic things hold the plants to the stakes.

Rob: Yeah, we didn't have enough and my kids didn't use them. Our plants were hard to get good measurements on.

The conversation continued with Mary and Rob sharing their expertise on the unit—what worked for them, what did not work for them, and what other activities they added to the unit. Their experience was positive and they shared these feelings with Ramona as well. I had been participating in some of Ramona's classes and the confidence that she heard from the other two teachers about the unit encouraged her to try many of the same activities that they found successful. My role with these teachers evolved to a participating learner as they shared with me their teaching experiences.

Researcher as Listener

It was from a willingness to listen to open-ended and complex verbalized analyses ... that I came to learn that such a conversational processes could provide the context for supporting all of our goals—the research team's need to study learning to teach and the beginning teachers' need for support to learn about complex classroom issues. I learned what teaching issues were raised, why they surfaced, how the teachers worked through and made sense of them—and the results of their sense-making. (Hollingsworth, p. 22)

In my conversations with the teachers about the curriculum, they began to share with me their concerns. Teachers shared successes with me: student science journals, student projects, stories about students and learning, books they had found on their topics, comments that children had made about science, and so forth. Teachers also shared concerns about the project. These concerns were mainly related to these questions: Would four units per grade level be enough? (Will there be enough variety? Will the pacing be too slow?) Will the students learn enough science content? How will we know if the kids are learning? How do we assess student learning? Will the kids do well on the state and achievement tests? How do we know that there will be an adequate scope and sequence? How do we assess kids working in groups? Will there be classroom management concerns? Who is going to manage the materials (keep the units organized and supplied)? Where does health[8] fit in? By creating spaces to listen to the teachers and in trying to understand the ways that these concerns and successes relate to one another, I can try to understand the ways the teachers are working to understand the process of teaching in their own minds. Their concerns seem mainly related to learning to teach processes and moving away from concentrating on content teaching. This is a change in the way that teachers may think about what it means to teach.

Researcher as Validator

To some teachers, I became a way for them to validate the ways that they were feeling as they interacted with the new curriculum. They utilized my recording as a way to make their voice heard. One example of this occurred as soon as I entered a third grade classroom. The students were out to recess and the teacher was straightening things up, getting ready for the science lesson that would take place upon their return in a few minutes. "Hi, David! How are things going?" I asked as I came in.

David smiled and said, "I want you to get this on tape." He went on to tell me that he thought that there was no way that the new science curriculum was going to work, how there was no way that the students could engage in the inquiry for a full nine weeks, that the school district's test scores are going to fall—which is the way that the community, the administrators, and the teachers judge their work.

> Number one, I'm scared for the test scores. I mean maybe some others are happy being on a third grade level, but we've always been on a fifth grade level. We have done well. We have so much to teach and I've already spent four weeks on this and it is doing, but I don't know what the kids are taking away. We have so much to cover. I've got the incubator, the experiments I promised the kids we could do and its not fun for me or for anybody when we're rushed. They don't know the vocabulary. I feel that they need a foundation before they do the hands on stuff for it to make any sense to them. And, in the last week they've gotten tired of it. I think today's lesson will be good because they get to compare the different rocks and minerals, but don't know what to do with myself. I don't feel like I'm teaching when the students are doing. They like it, but are they learning? I've tried to do the kit exactly as it is presented to really see what it is like and I feel like there needs to be a balance.

David went on to talk about how he did not feel that the curriculum direc-
tor really heard him when he expressed his concerns and that he just
needed to state the concerns that he had. It is evident in the way that
David talked about the new curriculum and that he had many concerns
that needed to be addressed if the new curriculum was going to play any
role in his science classes. My role as researcher here needed to be a
trusted listener. By hearing what David had to say, I tried to weave his
experience into my understanding of the process of implementing new
curriculum.

Researcher as Artist

In our work as researchers, we weigh and sift experiences, make choices
regarding what is significant, what is trivial, what to include, what to
exclude. We do not simply chronicle "what happened next," but place the
"next" in a meaningful context. By doing so, we craft narratives; we write
lives. (Richardson, 1990, p. 10)

As we piece together parts of the story, like the pieces of Bateson's
quilt, researchers become artists. The researcher makes decisions regarding the parts to leave in, the parts to take out, and how to frame and piece
together the narrative. Our own autobiography is a part of this creative
process. It shapes the ways that we come to a project, see a project, and
work on the project. Our experience shapes our interest and the construction of particular research and teaching interests (Connelly & Clandinin,
1995, p. 6).

My research interests come from my own personal experiences of working in schools, being a classroom teacher, creating curriculum, and collaborating with other teachers. As the impetus for my interests, I feel a part
of the conversations and stories I am researching. Developing and implementing curriculum are important, interesting, and worthy processes.
Because I have a personal connection to the research, from my past experiences and from the experiences I have had while working on this
project, I want to help be a part of the telling of these important, interesting and worthy stories about the processes of developing and implementing curriculum.

This personal influence and experience is not only a part of the writing
process, but begins as interest is created in a research project and then in
the ways that the story is collected. By establishing relationships with
teachers, by participating and observing in their classrooms, and by talking with the teachers, I began to frame my construction of the ongoing
story. Clandinin and Connelly talk about some of the ways of collecting
stories. Field notes are an "active recording." They suggest the ways in
which the researcher expresses her personal practical knowing in her

work. The term suggests that the notes are an active reconstruction of the events rather than a passive recording, that could have been recorded without the researcher's interpretation. Interviewing can also be a part of gathering stories. They are ways that both participants (the interviewer and the interviewed) come to "understand the narrative experiences shape their understanding of a particular text" (Clandinin & Connelly, 1992, pp. 5-6).

Bateson (1989) writes about the ways that she designed her narrative construction:

> This book is the outcome of a process of conversation and reflection. It is a way of making these lives available to others in a form that differs both from the extended narratives of heroic biography or case history on the one hand and the lost individuality of the survey on the other. These are not representative lives. They do not constitute a statistical sample--only, I hope, an interesting one. As I have worked over the material, I have become aware that the portions of these life histories that interest me the most ate the echoes from one life to another, the recurrent common themes. Teasing these out of a wealth of material and conversation and recognizing aspects of my own experience in different forms has been the process that I found personally most freeing and illuminating. (p. 16)

She comes back to this theme later in her book:

> No doubt they [the stories] are shaped again by my own selections, resonating variously with my own experience. These are stories I have used to think with, sometimes quoting at length and sometimes very briefly, sometimes approaching an issue almost entirely through the eyes of one woman and at other times lining them all up for comparison. (pp. 33-34)

The artistry that I have brought to this project has been ongoing. Decisions were made as I collected and analyzed the stories, saw how they related to one another, and how they could be woven together to contribute to an understanding of the ways that teachers work. Piece by piece, the quilt has come together, hopefully with a backing that holds it together and a pattern that is interesting and useful for both teachers and researchers.

Portraiture as a Narrative Method

Portraiture is a way to look at the research process and the writing of the narrative inquiry. It describes the way that I envision this book unfolding to the reader.

The portraits are designed to capture the richness, complexity, and dimensionality of the people who are negotiating those experiences. The portraits are shaped through dialogue between the portraitist and the subject, each one participating in the drawing of the image. (Lawrence-Lightfoot & Davis, 1997, p. 3)

But portraiture is more than a description of the experiences; it has a purpose. That purpose is to create a document "of inquiry *and* intervention, hopefully leading toward new understandings and insights, as well as instigating change" (p. 5). I hope that the chapters that follow will fulfill both of these goals: (1) to create a picture of the process of change through the individual narratives and (2) to bring new understandings and insights to the process of change.

NOTES

1. Names of the town, schools, and school staff are pseudonyms.
2. The committee was composed of 10 teachers who represent all grade levels, kindergarten through eighth grade.
3. Marilyn, Margery, and I had multiple roles as participants in the grant and the reform efforts. Marilyn Sinclair is a retired science teacher and district level science coordinator. Her role was mainly leading formal planning meetings, dealing with the administrative aspects of the grant and the district, and helping to set up the systems that keep the materials and supplies available for teachers. She also acted as the administrator of the Summer Science Camp and helped to teach the graduate course. Margery Osborne is a faculty member in the Department of Curriculum and Instruction at the University of Illinois at Urbana-Champaign. Margery's main role in the grant was teaching the summer graduate course and teaching a class of elementary students enrolled in the summer science camp. She was also an invaluable resource and support as we worked through the reform efforts in the classroom. In my role, I tried to support the teachers' efforts. I visited classrooms (as another set of hands, as a coteacher, as a participant in the lesson), I participated in planning sessions and meetings (both informal and formal), and I listened to the teachers and tried to act on their needs. I also taught an elementary class during the summer science camp and assisted with the teacher course.
4. During the 1998-1999 school year, 10 units were piloted. Fourteen teachers were involved in the teaching of these units. During the 1999-2000 school year, a total of 22 units were piloted. Later all teachers who taught science in the district elementary grades (K-6) were involved in the teaching (30 teachers).
5. Jan is one of the elementary teachers in Balmoral that I worked with. This incident occurred in the middle of the 1998-1999 school year.
6. I think these "roles" more clearly define the space I occupy as part of the process than the usual "participant-observer" label.
7. Many of the teachers did see me as an agent of change, which I will discuss in Chapter 5 among other issues of ownership in reform efforts.

8. Each grade level taught a sequence of science topics that most teachers followed from the table of contents in their science textbooks. Along with topics of science, the science texts also included topics of health (systems of the human body, effects of drugs on the human body, etc.). These health topics were not included in the suggested reforms. The district continued to discuss where the students would study the health curriculum.

CHAPTER 2

THE RESEARCH CONTEXT

BALMORAL, REFORM, AND STANDARDIZED TESTS

HAVE WE LEARNED THE THINGS TO PASS THE TEST?

It is the second year of the project, toward the end of the school year. I came to visit Elizabeth's classroom. The science activity and lesson today was the fertilization of her Wisconsin Fast Plants[1] with freeze-dried bees. The students had been studying the bees, their structures, and their place in the cycle of the plant's life. Today they would glue the bees to sticks and use the bees to move pollen from one plant to another. The actual freeze-dried bees were not necessary for this process (a cotton swab would do the job), but all of the teachers who had completed the activity with their classes felt that the bees were an interesting and worthwhile simulation as the students could take time to study the structures of the insects and actually see and imagine the process of fertilization as it might happen naturally. As I entered the classroom, Elizabeth was at the front of the room, looking very stern—something I had not seen often. She told me later that a child in her previous class had eaten one of the bees. She said she was stressed because there was so much going on. I thought that perhaps she was referring to the fact that the district achievement tests are next week. I asked her what she thought about the tests. She replied, "I've

---

Teachers and the Reform of Elementary Science, 27–49

got so much else going on! If I didn't have to pollinate the plants, finish the computer projects, and complete their novel projects, I'd have time to worry. It reminds me of that new Dr. Seuss book. Have you read it?" I had not and she described that it was a book about learning and not learning for a test, but learning so that the kids did well on the test because they learned to think. "I hope that's what is going on here!"

I went and bought the book, *Hurray for Diffendoofer Day!* (Seuss & Prelutsky, 1998). In the book, the students go to an unusual school where the teachers are "different-er." Dr. Seuss's idea for the book was to celebrate individuality and creative thinking. In his story these ideas are dampened at the school when the principal announces at lunch one day,

> All schools for miles and miles around
>
> Must take a special test,
>
> To see who's learning such and such—
>
> To see which school's the best.

The teacher in the book, the heroine, Miss Bonkers reassures her students,

> You've learned the things you need
>
> To pass that test and many more—
>
> I'm certain you'll succeed.
>
> We've taught you that the earth is round,
>
> That red and white make pink.
>
> And something else that matters more—
>
> We've taught you how to think.

Of course, in true Dr. Seuss fashion, the children and creative thinking prevail, making his point that children who learn to think will succeed no matter what kinds of restrictions tests seem to make on creativity and individual thinking. They celebrate as the school does the very best of all the schools around on the test.

I describe the book because I think that it sets the stage for the way that many of the teachers in Balmoral see the new science curriculum and pedagogy and the achievement tests. They want the students in their classes enjoy their learning and to be actively involved in the process of learning, but they also want the tests to continue to show (through high scores) that the students know what is expected by the state and their community. Again, there is an assumption here that the high test scores are equated with knowledge, prestige for the community, and a positive reputation for the schools, the teachers, and the administration. In this chapter, I will give a description of this community, which creates part of the context in which these teachers work.

The Dr. Seuss book also sets up a dichotomy of two cultures at work in educational reform, two cultures that we tried to synthesize: the culture of science education reform and the culture of standards and standardized testing. In this project we tried to support the efforts of teachers learning to implement national and state science education standards as they taught an activity-based science curriculum. Both sets of standards advocate similar philosophies in the ways that children should learn science. However, the teachers argued repeatedly that the tests that the children in their schools took (state tests based on the standards as well as an achievement test chosen by the district) do not reflect what the standards say. They believed that the tests were more fact-based and that an experience-based, limited-topic curriculum would not prepare the students for these tests. This chapter explores further the context of our work and these statements. In particular, I will describe the town of Balmoral, outline the ideas of the grant, and describe the goals of the tests. I will also attempt to show that these ideas formulate a culture that affects the ways that the state and local tests played a part in how the teachers viewed the science reform efforts. All of these ideas create a context in which the teachers worked to negotiate how the changes in pedagogy and in science curriculum were enacted in their classrooms.

A UNIQUE COMMUNITY: THE RESEARCH SITE

Balmoral, Illinois is like many small towns in central Illinois. With a population of around 5,000, it is surrounded by farmland, has a central town square with a courthouse in the middle. Antique, craft, and drugstores intermingle with restaurants to encircle the courthouse. There are also art galleries and flower shops on the square. The rest of the business district directly surrounds the square and includes farm supply shops and other agriculturally related businesses like the grain elevator and farm insurance companies. There are the typical fast food restaurants and chain gas station stop and shops. One intersection controls the flow of traffic with a brand new stoplight, the installation of which was the subject of heated debate. Possibly because of this, people in the area often use this intersection as the main point of reference when giving directions. "Turn left at *the* traffic light." The town itself seems very pleasant—it is generally quite, clean and well kept. Balmoral is growing. Until recently, it was hard to find housing if someone wanted to move into Balmoral. This need has been addressed with several new housing developments being built on the edges of the town. In town, the houses are of a mixed variety. Evidence of old money abounds but newer, more modest homes are present also. There are older Victorian mansions along the main street, newer clapboard and brick homes, older housing developments, as well as trailer parks. There are several nature parks in town and in the surrounding county. Tourist information lists the town's theater group, its interest in the arts, and its "great schools." In fact, almost any information about the town begins with a reference to the excellent schools. "Just about everyone in these parts knows what a fine community Balmoral is: nice homes on tree-lined streets, a great downtown, good recreation facilities, easy access, a strong school system, a nice library, a low crime rate and even lower taxes" (Kacich, 2000).

Balmoral is also unlike many small towns in central Illinois because of several influences in its growth and development that have played a part in creating the town. Balmoral has a unique history and that history has had a great impact on the town that Balmoral is today. The sign on the side of the road as I exit the interstate and drive into the town says "welcome to Balmoral." A welcome sign is not unusual, but the symbol of the town on the sign says "unique." And, the symbols of the town on the sign are unique. The town symbol holds a comedy and tragedy mask, a painter's palette, a storefront, golf club and ball, a sculpture, and a railway train engine and depot, and a children's park. These symbols allude to the past, the influences that have played and continue to play a part in creating the atmosphere of the town, the place that is Balmoral. The arts and industry have both contributed to the kinds of things that the community values and support, that people coming to Balmoral expect and find. The chamber of commerce flyer promotes the town:

> You can leave traffic lights behind and go back to tree-lined streets, top-notch schools, a library filled with volumes of knowledge, a town square buzzing from discussions of lawyers and clients, charming homes and bountiful gardens, numerous stores, a hospital, clinics, child care centers known for meticulous and tender care, parks for fun, a planned retirement village, and people willing to get involved.

This interesting juxtaposition of progressive attitudes as well as traditional expectations makes Balmoral its own unique place.

History of this Unique Place

The Balmoral area was settled and became the county seat in the 1840s. Before White settlers took over the land and used it for cattle grazing, the land was inhabited by the Kickapoo and Pottawatomie tribes of the Algonquin Indians. In the 1850s railroads brought easier transportation to the town and a change from mainly livestock farming to grain farming. Many of the large homes in town were built around the turn of the century when patent medicine created a boom industry in Balmoral. This boom led to the construction of mansions along State Street dubbed "Millionaire's Row." "There were at one time more millionaires in Balmoral than in any other town of its size in the world" (West, 1966). After the crash of the stock market in 1929, banking, the hospital, and the agricultural and related businesses kept Balmoral growing.

One of the most interesting millionaires whose ties with the town continue even today, was a man named Samuel Allerton. His estate, which is today Allerton Park, lies outside of town. Allerton's son Robert took over the management of the 12,000 acre farm, but also collected reproductions of art from around the world and showcased the works in manicured gardens around the estate. Robert Allerton gave the park and several hundred acres of farmland to provide for its maintenance to the University of Illinois in 1946. The artwork, the river, prairie, and wooded landscape, and fact that the park is adjacent to the state 4-H camp make Allerton park a very interesting place. This interest has built a strong connection between the park and Balmoral. People in the area associate the two together which also creates part of the towns identity.

The community has few minorities, high socioeconomic factors, and a history of the community's connection to art, drama, and "gracious living" (West, 1966). The community also has a history of traditional midwestern farming and agricultural industries. The community has had an interest in the school system and continues to support it with high expectations.

Balmoral Schools

The school district encompasses a large part of the county, with many of the students riding buses to school. The high school and middle school are located in Balmoral along with one grade school. Jefferson Grade School houses grades kindergarten through grade four. Two other nearby communities also send their children to these schools and another grade school with grades kindergarten through six is located in one of those towns. One hundred percent of the teachers are White, and 99% of the students are White. Thirteen percent of the students are eligible for free or reduced lunch (Illinois School Report Card, 1998).

It is generally known that the town has a very high tax base to rely on for funding its public schools. At one time two large utility companies incorporated within the city and they paid their personal property taxes in Balmoral even though their actual headquarters were located in the larger Illinois communities of Decatur and Bloomington. The taxing districts in Balmoral including the school district received millions of dollars. The community still receives funds from corporate taxes paid to the state in the form of a state replacement tax that is paid since the dropping of the state personal property tax in the 1970s. The money from those replacement taxes was enacted to keep the taxing districts afloat if a large corporation moved from the community. It continues to help keep the local property taxes low (Kacich, 2000). The school board has made commitments to keeping class sizes low, hiring teaching assistants, and including special teachers for reading and "Reading Recovery" programs in the elementary grades. The district also has full time computer teachers in each building along with an art teacher and music teacher. The schools have a positive reputation and one teacher told me, "People move here because of the school district's reputation."

Many of the teachers in the grade school live and or even grew up in the area. The teachers generally are veteran teachers as the district average for the number of years taught is 16 years (Illinois School Report Card, 1998). Many have spent their entire careers teaching in this school district. Their children go to the schools, play in the marching band, on the football and softball teams, and are in their colleagues' classrooms. There seems to be a sense of pride in the town and the schools. The teachers are proud to work in these schools. They like the successes that they have had and want to keep their standards high. "The district goal is to have less than 10% of our students that do not meet performance standards and to have at least 35% that exceed standards in all areas of the IGAP" (Illinois School Report Card, 1998).

Like many communities, Balmoral publishes its state test scores in the local paper. A local paper rated the Balmoral school district the highest of 46 area school districts. It based the rating on the annual school report cards mandated by the state. The scores on the state mandated tests have been above average with over 90% of the students meeting or exceeding the state performance standards and all of the district scores exceeding the state averages in all subjects (Illinois School Report Card, 1998). These scores seem to give the community, the teachers, and the school administration a sense of pride in their schools and their work.

Throughout the time that I spent working with the teachers in various ways on the science project, these test scores became a constant part of conversations. The issue of keeping their district scores high was an important aspect of evaluating their performance as teachers, their pride in their work, and their reputation as a "very good" school district. This issue of reputation and what constitutes a positive reputation is an issue that requires a closer examination. What constitutes a "good reputation" for a school district? The answer to this depends on the community in which it is situated. Balmoral is a very White, very middle class, very traditional community which holds very traditional expectations for their students. In talking with the teachers, a good school is one that prepares its students to do further study and to know skills which will help them contribute to their community. Part of this is doing well on tests as these open the doors to further education and also a sense of pride in their work. Since the district has already provided this to the community, as shown by the consistently high test scores, why would the teachers want to chance jeopardizing what is already working? Why rock the boat? The status quo supports a general consensus of what a "good school" does. The status quo has provided high test scores, why change? The teachers generally accepted the idea that they were changing the science curriculum[2] and instead of asking "why change?" they began the work of finding ways to make the changes comfortable or workable for them in the context of their individual classrooms.

Learning and the Science Curriculums

I want to briefly discuss the two science curriculums, what I call the "old curriculum" and the "new curriculum." In the old curriculum, the teachers used a series of textbooks which had four basic overarching units: Earth Science, Life Science, Physical Science and Health. In each grade level the students studied content related to these units as individual chapters in their science texts. This was what the teachers followed as their main science curriculum. In the text, the science content, or facts, was seen as the focus of the learning. Many teachers added in the suggested activities or those activities and lessons of their own design to support the textbook content. It was this practice that lead to discussion for changing the science curriculum. Some teachers saw a need for a more activity and process-based curriculum and others saw a need for a more focused science study—one that did not overlap between grade levels. As I described in Chapter 1, initial meetings of a science committee led to the project of changing the science curriculum.

The new curriculum was based on activities and on science process or inquiry skills. These are skills that are used while doing a scientific activity and are "abilities that help people gain information about nature and natural phenomena: observing, inferring, classifying, recording data, predicting, and planning investigations" (Koch, 1999, p. 375). In this type of curriculum the focus of study is on learning and applying those skills to solve a problem or find an answer to a question. Scientific facts and content are learned while doing the investigation or in conjunction with the investigation to support the learning. The two curriculums really have different views of the ways that children learn and understand their world. Feinberg (1998, p. 30) explores the "question of meaning and how it is to be taught." He writes in response to Hirsch (1998) who states that meaning is learned by rote, a brute fact, and that these facts will provide the foundation for active learning. This is

> a transmission view of meaning and reinforces, intentionally or not, tell and tally educational practices. Teachers hold meaning in their heads, and their job is to transmit it in the most efficient way to the head of the student. Whole class instruction, telling (which can include story telling), and rote memorization are frequently seen as the most effective means for accomplishing this exchange, and standardized tests are the most effective way to tally how well the task has been accomplished. (Feinberg, 1998, p. 30)

This transmission view of teaching and learning was the old curriculum. The students learned the information in the text as a foundation for the science that they would do in later grades. With this curriculum the students had fared well on the state and local standardized tests.

The new curriculum could be seen as a more transactional way of learning and understanding. Again from Feinberg,

> This view takes meaning as a social activity.... Meaning is not an isolated string of brute facts that one head implants in another. It is shaped in the context of doing with others.
>
> Meaning serves to organize and coordinate activity toward some end or purpose. It is a doing, and that doing also entails the specialized *doings* that we call *reading, listening, talking,* and *writing.* These forms of interaction enable us to be conscious of our purposes and to reflect on them and, when appropriate, to change them. (Feinberg, 1998, p. 31)

In science learning the doings are also observing, inferring, classifying, recording data, predicting, and planning investigations. Children make sense and create meaning about their world through these doings rather than through learning facts. For example, by creating experiments to test the needs of a plant (amount of light, water, nutrients, space, etc.) students will make their own sense of how a plant's needs affect its growth. This is the philosophy of the new curriculum—a philosophy that differs greatly from the transmission view of learning. They portray two different ideas about the nature of what is worthwhile for children to learn in science (received knowledge versus constructed knowledge) and also about what is the nature of science. These differing philosophies about the ways that children gain understanding was part of the underlying tension of changing curriculums for the Balmoral teachers. It is the question of what knowledge is worth teaching? (Kliebard, 1975/1997). This tension manifested itself in the ways that teachers saw the reforms, in the ways that they related the reforms to the standardized tests and their colleagues, and in the ways that they enacted the ideas of reform in their classrooms.

CONVERSATIONS ABOUT REFORM AND CONVERSATIONS ABOUT STANDARDS: CREATING TENSION

As I am writing this, a political debate plays in the background. The issue being discussed is education—the crisis in education, the failures of our educational system and what each of the candidates would do to improve the failure of the system. "High standards, high expectations, testing to make sure these standards are met," I hear one of the candidates say. The local paper recently ran a series of reports on the state tests. The Sunday headline on the front page read "A Tale of Two Schools: How kids from vastly different neighborhoods face challenge of standardized tests" (Ryckman, 2000). In a local "educational" toy store I found on the bookshelf books directed towards parents of young children titled "Parents Guide to Testing" and "Parents Guide to Standards." From the standards book:

> Will standards improve education? To achieve a good education, all students should learn and perform at high levels. To keep our students competitive and to get the most from our investment in education, most states have adopted rigorous expectations for what students should able to do. By providing students, parents, and teachers with clear and consistent expectations across all of our schools, we increase the likelihood that students will perform at even higher levels than they have in the past. With the adoption of standards, the focus of education becomes not just what teachers teach but also what students learn. (Strabanek, 1998, p. 5)

This paragraph and the fact that these issues are so prevalent in the minds of the media, parents, and our society shows the ways that a "culture of testing" is part of the fabric of our schools.

When I say "culture" I am describing "socially transmitted behavior, patterns, arts, beliefs, institutions, and all other products of human work and thought characteristics of a community or population" (*American Heritage Dictionary*, p. 348). Erickson (1997) defines culture as a construction, "[A]ll thoughts, feelings, and human activity are not simply natural, but are the result of historical and personal experience that becomes sedimented as culture and in habit." In Balmoral both of these definitions of culture were at play. The teachers felt the pressure of keeping the status quo as that stasis had given them the high test scores. Their text-based curriculum which imparted science knowledge through the learning of science content and facts became a socially transmitted behavior and belief about learning and what was expected in their classrooms. The main impetus for this transmitted belief about learning and teaching was the teachers' perception of the community's expectations for their schools—an expectation strongly based on high standardized test scores. But, teachers also construct their own beliefs about teaching and learning. These constructions take place as they teach, as they reflect, as they experience successes and failures in the classroom, and as they try out activities and learning themselves. The personal experiences of teaching and learning and the community expectations of teaching at learning were at play as the Balmoral teachers worked through science curricular and pedagogical reforms.

In the realm of educational reform there is a focus on the ideas of standards and standardized testing that impact the ways that reform efforts are enacted in classrooms. There is a history of the impact of the test scores, the expectations of the community, and the ideas of what teaching and learning are. Those all impact the culture of the school. Geertz (1973) contends that we can see the culture in the routine ways that the members of the group (in this case the teachers in a particular school) act and make sense of ideas. As the Balmoral teachers made sense of the new science curriculum and how it would look in their own classrooms, the standards and standardized tested played a part in many of their understandings. How would the changes impact their scores? How will I know what the kids have learned? When Liston and Zeichner (1996) talk about "culture" they are not using it to specifically talk about standards and testing, however, the ideas that they use to talk about what "culture" means can be used to inform the idea that there is a culture of standards and standardized testing. These in turn impact reform efforts in education today, and more specifically the reform efforts in Balmoral:

> If we begin with the simple assumption that culture involves a set of meanings and meaning systems that people create and attach to their everyday lives and activities, and that teaching entails the facilitation and articulation of students' meaning systems, then we have before us a very large task indeed. (Liston & Zeichner, 1996, p. xvii)

What is the role of the teacher? How do we decide whose culture will be facilitated? Is there a common culture? (p. xvii) These are questions that can be directed to the creation of the standards movement and the context in which teachers are teaching. How are these standards created and whose knowledge do they promote? What is the teacher's role in interpreting them in their classrooms? Do the standardized tests reflect what we believe about teaching and learning? The current standards movement (which can also be seen as its own culture) contributes to school culture as it impacts the ways that teachers see meaning, learning, and teaching. A culture of testing impacted the ways the Balmoral teachers viewed the changes in the science curriculum. As teachers made decisions about how and what to teach in their classrooms, the idea of the tests became a common concern.

This current standards-based movement might be traced back to 1983 when *A Nation at Risk* appeared. This report "launched an attack on dumb teachers, uncaring mothers, social promotion, and general academic permissiveness" (Meier, 2000, p. 9). The report criticized our public school systems and implied that America was at large economic risk because schools were not preparing students adequately. The report blamed teachers and according to the report, which gave a large list of recommendations on content, standards, time devoted to learning basics, teaching, and leadership and fiscal support, "American education needed to be reimagined, made more rigorous, and above all, brought under the control of experts who, unlike educators and parents, understood the new demands of our economy and culture" (p. 10). After 20 years, the impact of this report is still being felt by teachers as they make pedagogical and curricular decisions in their classrooms. Teachers feel the pressure of being accountable for the learning that happens in their classrooms, learning that is measured by tests required and emphasized in this "culture."

> Across the land teachers are bowing to the pressure of corporate-politico-infotainment pronouncements: They are eliminating recess and putting away the building blocks, the tempra paints, and the picture books.... They are bringing out the skill drill worksheets that will get every kid in America learning the schwa on schedule. (Ohanian, 1999, p. 19)

I am not arguing that teachers should not be accountable for what goes on in their classrooms, nor that we should not have standards. I am arguing that standards and the standardized tests created to measure if teachers are doing their job should not be the driving force behind how and why teachers make decisions. I was surprised at the impact that this "culture of testing" played during the reform efforts promoted by this science literacy grant in Balmoral.

Between the Culture of Change and the Culture of Testing: Negotiating a Space to Teach Science

"We are done with the unit and hitting reviewing real hard for the achievement tests." David replied to my e-mail asking if a visit the following week would work in his schedule. His e-mail stated that they were practicing for the tests, covering material he felt they needed—information that was not covered in the third grade science curriculum. What makes David react to the tests in this manner—feeling that he needs to make sure that the kids are prepared, where the sixth grade teacher (the teacher I described earlier) felt that they would be prepared? Both teachers were teaching from the new curriculum. These teachers' own views of learning and teaching are different and the ways that they interpret the curriculums they teach are enacted in different ways in their classrooms. David feels that kids need "background knowledge before they can understand the processes." He is learning to be a facilitator instead of a transmitter of this knowledge and he is working on these skills in his classroom. He had to be convinced that he and his students could do things in a different way and continue to learn. Elizabeth, the sixth grade teacher, feels that the kids will be prepared by their experience, but still thinks that the tests are far more traditional than the science that the students have been participating and learning. In other words these tests are not process oriented, but lean more toward testing students on their factual knowledge of science. The perception of the tests by the teacher creates part of the shaping of the curricular and pedagogical change that occurs or does not occur in their individual classrooms.

> In my view one of the greatest obstacles is the fierce concentration on standardized tests of reading and arithmetic. It is not a concentration on reading and arithmetic per se that gets in the way.... But the concentration in schools today is not on reading and arithmetic. It is on standardized tests of reading and arithmetic, which is quite a different matter. None of the work here could be appreciated on a standardized test ... including science in the elementary curriculum does not interfere with the teaching of reading and arithmetic. On the contrary, it compliments and supports this teaching. What it does interfere with is practicing for standardized tests of reading and arithmetic, which take little account of the long term or the broad scope of learning. It is the grip of these standardized tests that so limits the ways teachers and children spend their time in elementary schools. One, among many, of the victims is science education. (Duckworth, 1990, pp. 23-24)

Although there is a matching of the goals in the statements of purpose of the tests and of the standards, the culture that these kinds of tests help promote undermines the synthesis that could occur. The tests could be used in ways to promote children learning in inquiry-based and creative thinking ways, but this is not the way that teachers interpret the goals of the tests. The tests are used to compare students against themselves, to show parents how well or not so well their children are achieving and also for students' placement in special programs (or as part of the process). But unless the assessment matches what is being taught in the classroom, then it is really not an assessment of school learning, nor should it be a driving force in making curricular and pedagogical decisions.

What children learn and the ways that teachers set up learning in their classrooms are topics that have been discussed for decades in our public schools. Dewey (1916/1944, p. 155) asks,

> Is the experience a personal thing of such nature as inherently to stimulate and direct observation of the connections involved, and to lead to inference and its testing? Or is it imposed from without, and is the pupil's problem simply to meet the external requirement?

Where should the stimulus for learning come from? What is the role of the teacher? How does learning become meaningful for children? The meaning is made in the way the subject matter is experienced by the learner (Dewey, 1916/44; Duckworth, 1972). This is the philosophy reflected in both the national and state science standards (American Association for the Advancement of Science, 1989, 1993; National Research Council, 1996; Illinois State Board of Education [ISBE], 2000). By making children familiar with their world in such a way as to "capture their interest, to let them raise and answer their own questions, to let them realize what they can do ... [teachers can give them tools] so that they have the interest, the ability, and the self-confidence to go on by themselves" (Duckworth, 1972, p. 225). To do this teachers need to feel that they have the freedom to diverge from their plans—to value the questions and insights that they and their students make along the way of their teaching and learning. "If teachers feel that their class must do things just as the book says, and that their excellence as a teacher depends upon that, they cannot possibly accept children's divergence and children's creations" (Duckworth, 1972, p. 225). How can children be taught to think, to question, and to problem solve, if the goals and objectives of the lessons are so specifically stated that they seem to stifle creative teaching and learning? When the teachers ask me, "How will the kids score on the state test?" it is that feeling that the kids must do exactly as the book says to know if they came away with the lesson goal that leads them to this dissonance.

State performance and locally chosen achievement tests create an atmosphere of teaching to a specified list of facts, of uncreative thinking, and narrow viewpoints. When school districts and communities demand and expect that the evidence of their school's and teacher's performance is based on a report in the paper, then teachers and school feel a pressure to teach so that their students will perform well on these tests. What kinds of teaching and thinking does this encourage? It is not surprising that teachers are concerned with how and what they teach will affect their test scores. The real question is, if we value thinking, creative problem solving, and varying viewpoints, why do we continue to put such emphasis on the tests as an evaluation of our public schools? These questions are seen in popular media, in national political debates, and in local newspapers. A recent *Newsweek* cover story was devoted to the subject of testing students and evaluating students and schools. "[The state tests] are the law and as a consequence they're beginning to drive the curriculum. We spend a lot more time teaching to the test and a lot less on the kind of hands on, learn-by-doing teaching we did in the past" (McGinn, 1999, p. 50). In response to a question about judging a school's effectiveness through test scores, Theodore Sizer states, "You can hide in a test. You can't hide in an inspection.... Tests are an easy out. They have a facade of toughness and objectivity. Tests put no burden on the people who most often demand them—the politicians" (Kantowitz, 1999, p. 51). The teachers feel the burden. This is the burden that many of the teachers trying the new science curriculum feel. They want to understand for themselves that this is the "right" thing to do, that a curriculum based on the processes of learning is the best way to teach science. Following their journey—their individual negotiation of these two seemingly opposing contexts within the change process—is an important way to see how their individual stories impact the district-wide curriculum and pedagogical reforms.

Several of the teachers have expressed concern about the how their classes will do on these tests. David, a third grade teacher, continually asked questions and began to make adjustments in his teaching to fulfill his own need to fit the new curriculum into his own understanding of his role as science teacher. "I am definitely more of a guide now. I've added a few vocabulary words that we've read about and we are going to have the students identify the rocks and minerals by name because I feel that the parents want them to be accountable and I do, too! Without these things it is hard to evaluate the students. How do you evaluate thinking skills and how much hands-on is tested on the achievement tests?" David questioned the best way to evaluate what the children in his class had learned, what consisted of "learning" to him and to his parents. Both of the answers to the questions in his mind both came back to the proof that the achievement tests would show and what he wanted to show the community through the scores on those tests.

David and I had been watching the students create pulley systems. As we walked around the classroom, we interacted with the groups of students learning to use force in the most efficient way and asked them questions about what they had been doing. After class, David told me that he felt the kids really understood what they were doing, but did not believe that their knowledge would be shown on an achievement test by these activities, discussions, and writing about the pulley systems they had created. He stated that the tests asked about vocabulary and used diagrams that kids could not experiment with to find the correct answer. He felt he needed to expose them to the "test kind of learning" otherwise he was not being fair to them. It was important to him to be able to keep up the test scores for them, for the community and school's reputation, and also for his own reputation and piece of mind as an effective teacher.

Karen, another third grade teacher, continued to struggle with the tension she experienced from the changes. "I understand that there isn't always a right way to do things or a right answer to the questions probed. The more I do the science myself, the more I feel confident about the science program. It [the science teaching and learning] is more interesting. I really like this science program, but the gripe that I have had all along is that it has to be done right. If you don't have enough time to do it right, the kids miss out on learning. Hands-on learning doesn't lend itself to fitting science into a half hour block like working out of a book might. With everything that I have to cover for the tests, the pressure to make sure that students get all the information makes me worry that I'm not getting it all in." Karen does not see the goals of the inquiry science program fitting with the realities of teaching and learning—time constraints, expectations of state and local standards, and her own understanding of what teaching and learning science are.

When this school district made the public commitment to make changes in its pedagogical processes and its curriculum through the state science literacy grant, Balmoral schools also made a commitment in time, finances, and effort in promoting change and ongoing in-service for its teachers. The school district also continues to give the state and local tests to assess student achievement and progress toward state and local goals for learning. Both of these ideas—change in pedagogy and curriculum and giving standardized tests—created a tension in the minds of the teachers as they worked to implement science reforms within their individual classrooms. Most of the teachers liked the ideas of the changes, but also felt a reality of the way the tests reflected on their students, teaching, and their school. Negotiation of the two cultures, how to find a balance that they could be comfortable with became the enactment and the individual realities of the science reform efforts.

A Context of Reform: Achievement Tests and State Science Tests

The achievement test that Balmoral schools give is the Stanford Achievement Test (1996). I listened to the teachers talk about the test during the two years that I worked with them, saying things like "These are the topics that are covered on the test. I don't know where these are in our new curriculum. Especially, when they've only covered a few units by the time they take some of these tests in the earlier grades. And by the time we give these tests during the school year, we have only covered two topics." From the comments I heard, I would not have thought that these excerpts came from the introduction to the science portion of the achievement test:

> The Stanford 9 Science subtest is designed to assess understanding in the domains of life, physical, and earth sciences. Mirroring the philosophy presented in Science for All Americans, the Science subtest de-emphasizes specific content vocabulary and emphasizes the unifying themes and concepts of science. The same criteria used in the drafts of the National Science Education Standards were employed to determine the importance of conceptual information. These criteria include the ideas that the concept should have strong predictive power, be applicable in many situations, guide observation, encourage questioning, and represent organizing principles.

The introduction goes on to state,

> The science portion of the subtest provides an overview of children's understanding of common experiences in the natural environment. Questions reflect understanding of general concepts more than the specific details of science.... As much as possible, the concepts are developmentally appropriate conforming to the concepts outlined in the Benchmarks for Science Literacy.... Test items allow students to use reasoning skills to reach answers rather than recall memorized, detailed information. Students may be asked to apply an understanding of the concept directly to a situation, but, more often, they are asked to use these concepts to interpret data, draw conclusions, and predict events. The habits of the mind skills described in Science for All Americans form the foundation of the reasoning skills students are asked to use throughout the subtest. These skills include estimating, making simple calculations, seeking patterns, making observations, recognizing cause and effect, reading standard instruments, and drawing conclusions.

The state of Illinois requires that school districts give the Illinois Standards Achievement Tests (ISAT) in science at grades 4 and 7. The tests are based on the Illinois Learning Standards and the tests assess (1) methods of inquiry; (2) life sciences; (3) physical sciences; (4) earth and space sciences; and (5) science, technology, and society. The state lists the purposes of the ISAT science tests,

> to measure each student's overall science achievement; measure each student's achievement with respect to the five standard sets; provide information as to how schools, districts, and the state are performing in science; monitor science progress of students, schools, and districts and the state

over time; and generate information on science achievement that can be used for accountability, policy-making and school improvement.

The tests are used for purposes of accountability for the districts and schools to the state as well as to local communities.

The Illinois State Board of Education also gives suggestions for school, teacher, and student preparation. "The science goals and standards should be an integral part of a district's science program at all grades.... Good preparation occurs when a district aligns its local objectives in science with the state standards and modifies its curriculum, instruction, tests, and remedial actions on the basis of test results." This is where the some of the teachers saw a disconnect in the changing of Balmoral's science program. They saw that their districts test scores were high, that it seemed that the students and the schools were meeting the requirements of the state so why was there a reason to change? Changing curriculum and pedagogies can be difficult work and can also create more work for teachers, especially if they do not believe that there is a good reason or believe in the change themselves.

The state goes further to state that the purpose of the ISAT test,

> unlike some standardized tests ... is not to measure the quantity of students' memories, but the quality of their thinking—*whether they can think as a scientist* ... instruction that requires students to memorize huge volumes of static, disconnected names or esoteric facts is poor preparation for the ISAT. On the other hand, instruction that focuses on asking why, learning dynamic principles, mastering the norms and logic of scientific inquiry, interpreting data from graphs and tables, understanding the implications of technology upon society and applying technology upon society and applying a fundamental principles to problems is excellent preparation.

These are the kinds of ideas that the grant written to support the district in changing its science curriculum tried to support. The grant was written to synthesize the ideas of science reform efforts and also the requirements of the state science standards. In writing these ideas seem to align themselves and match up.

S. A. G. E. S.: *"Science as Guided by Education Standards"*

The following sections will describe in detail the goals of the grant and the activities outlined in the grant to meet those objectives. I do not explain these ideas in detail as a basis for evaluation of this project, but to show more of the context in which we were working. This book is a description and analysis of what went on in Balmoral as we tried to follow the guidelines set in the grant. It is a study of what happened in this context. As the title of the state grant for scientific literacy states, this grant was based on science education standards. The grant was written in conjunction with the university to support teachers and the district in making major and sustainable systematic changes in the implementation of an improved science program (ISBE grant, 1999, p. 2). Before writing the grant, a university professor (Margery) and a science education consultant (Marilyn) met with district administrators and members of a science committee to find out what the needs of the district were. In surveying the teachers of the district, the group wrote in the grant a summary of the needs of the Balmoral teachers:

1. Opportunities to increase their knowledge of fundamental concepts and principles of science, and to experience learning science through problem solving, communication of information and ideas, using teamwork and appropriate technology.
2. Opportunity to sharpen their pedagogical skills for teaching inquiry science, and to practice applying those skills in the classroom.
3. Support and guidance in the design of a science curriculum that provides the students opportunities to become knowledgeable of appropriate science concepts and principles, and the processes and applications of science.
4. Assistance in developing more authentic methods of assessing student performance skills and their understanding of content at the conceptual level.
5. Assistance in the evaluation of the effectiveness of the curriculum and pedagogical practices on student learning and attitudes within the science disciplines (ISBE grant, 1999, p. 2)

With these needs in mind and with the main goal of the program outlined in the grant to "provide quality and sustained guidance and expertise to the personnel of the Balmoral Schools in order to improve the district's science program"(ISBE, 1999, p. 3), the district's aims are to give students opportunities to understand fully the inquiry processes of science, fundamental concepts and principles of science, and social issues related to science and technology (p. 3). Based on this major goal the grant states three objectives which outline the structural supports to help teachers understand for themselves the reform efforts thoroughly and give them opportunities to try out, reflect on, and make changes in the new curriculum and pedagogy. Because these objectives are a summary of how the grant became enacted and also an explanation of the ways that the university and the school district worked together, I want to take some space here to outline the objectives and the realities of the ways that those objectives were enacted. In other words, I will describe the things that we did to try to meet these objectives.

Objective One: Staff Development.   The teachers made it clear that they wanted more knowledge in content appropriate for elementary classrooms and also that they needed knowledge of how to teach science in a process-based program. By setting up a graduate level course designed for the teachers in the Balmoral district, teachers were given an opportunity to learn about science inquiry through their own learning experience. The course was set up for the teachers to do science themselves the first two weeks of the class. The teachers explored science content in a classroom environment that tried to model the type of science teaching being recommended for student learning of science concepts. They worked in cooperative learning groups and participated in an inquiry-process approach to teaching and learning science. Then the teachers worked in collegial pairs to try out the curriculum and pedagogy on a small class of children who were enrolled in their own two-week science camp during the second two weeks of the course. These teams were set up for collaboration and support.

During the science camp with elementary students, the teachers came together following each day's sessions with students for the purpose of reflecting on their learning, the students learning, and issues of supplies, routines, and so forth. Teachers also kept a journal of their experiences with some guided questions and other general reflections. Teachers who participated in the summer course seemed much more confident in their abilities to teach with an inquiry approach and also in the merits of this approach during the school year. These teachers were often the first to pilot units. Some of the comments about the summer program from participating teachers included things like, "Science was fun for the kids and me. Writing and reporting their findings was not a labor for the kids, they were so excited about what they were doing." Other teachers who did not participate in the camp were effected by what they heard. "She's just real excited about the unit. I'm anxious to try it." From the grant renewal form,

> We believe that this summer program is an integral aspect of the process of changing the curriculum. The summer course offered teachers a risk-free, non-threatening environment to try the conceptual-inquiry approach to teaching. It also gave them a concrete experience of "doing' and provided a framework for understanding. (ISBE, 2000, p. 2)

Objective Two: On-going Guidance and Support.   This objective addressed the ongoing need for staff development. Change is not made through a meeting one afternoon and then going back to the classroom and implementing a program. By promoting ongoing staff development, the conversation of the reform efforts continued throughout the two-year cycle. This staff development would concentrate on current recommendations for school science programs and student learning (inquiry- and process-based approaches) and then on the design, implementation, and evaluation of curriculum for the Balmoral district. Formal meetings and workshops were scheduled for the science committee and for grade level groups. Informally, teachers also met after school or during planning times to discuss the curriculum and pedagogy—problems, solutions, and ideas for integrating the science with other subjects. Teachers also met at the completion of units to reflect on their teaching practices and on the units themselves. In addition to reflecting on their own practices, teachers communicated their experiences to teachers who had not yet piloted the units. As I visited classrooms, I also had conversations with teachers about the changes and their experiences. Information gathered from all of these formal and informal conversations was used for the purpose of directing future planning sessions and staff development as well as for making evaluations of the science curriculum and the effectiveness of the science curriculum and teaching methods by the teachers.

A variety of teaching materials were made available to the teachers during many of the planning sessions. We met at a nearby science center and the "experience of becoming familiar with sources beyond the traditional science textbook (school district curriculum guides, commercially and teacher prepared materials, children's literature, trade books, periodicals, etc.) helped teachers envision how they could develop an inquiry and process oriented curriculum for their students. These materials became support materials for the teachers as they gathered information used to design a science program to meet the specific needs of the Balmoral School District and to meet the recommendations of the Illinois State Board of Education" (ISBE, 2000).

Objective Three: Sufficient Resources and Supplies.   In a process-based science program supplies beyond a traditional textbook are used to provide students with learning experiences. The grant provided funds for single copies of resource materials to be purchased and collected as a "professional science library." This library consisted of books and resources requested by teachers as they designed and implemented the curriculum.

As teaching topics were chosen and the units designed, they were piloted in at least two classrooms. Then after conversation and reflection among the grade level teachers, changes, suggestions, and concerns were addressed and in all cases the units were implemented throughout the district. The grant provided supplies for two units per grade level per year to be piloted.

Alignment or Dichotomy?

I spend so much space discussing these standards, goals, objectives, and in the case of the grant, strategies for approaching the goals and objectives, because these are the ideas that gave us (teachers, administrators, and university personnel) the background for choosing the curriculum and the changes in the science curriculum. The first time that we met with grade-level groups we spent at least half of an in-service day discussing and going through the standards applicable to each grade level, both national and state standards. These are the ideas that are behind science education reform and also the ideas which set the context for these teachers' work. It is very interesting to me to note that these standards (both the national and state), the goals of the tests (both state and the locally chosen achievement tests), and the goals and objectives of the grant all are parallel in their philosophies and goals. All of the sets of standards state that learning science should be a process-oriented experience, promoting science content through inquiry skills and that the focus should be on the doing and discussing rather than on memorizing specific science content and facts. But, instead of seeing that as a powerful reason to make reforms, many of the teachers questioned whether these entities (the standards and the curriculum and pedagogy) were aligned.

This has been a description of many of the factors which create the context in which the teachers worked. I believe it is important to understand where these teachers were situated and understand that it was not a static situation. As the teachers worked with the changes and tried to find ways to make the changes work for their own understandings of teaching and learning, these understandings also changed. "The relationships between context and teachers' curriculum work, then, are neither unidirectional or static, but interactive and evolving over time … [It] must be treated as an integral and changing component of teachers' curriculum work" (Paris, 1993, p. 43). Where teachers are situated shapes the ways that they make sense of their experiences; the context plays a part in the ways that teachers see the changes and fit the changes into their own understandings of teaching and learning.

NO TIME FOR WONDERING

Marilyn was trying to find out what the teachers had gained or thought about the week we had spent investigating ecosystems and individual parts of ecosystems at her home. During the summer graduate course on inquiry, we met at Marilyn's house. It is situated on a bluff above the Sangamon River and is a setting that lends itself to discovering about nature. It also lends itself to a learning environment that is much more inviting than a classroom situation. Throughout the week I watched and interacted with the teachers as they sat in small groups on the pond dock, under the oak tree, or on a walk through the woods or digging in compost. The teachers also explored aspects of the natural prairie, Marilyn's herb and flower gardens, and her husband's vegetable garden. Groups of teachers also gathered on her screened in porch to look through books full of information and ideas related to their own questions and interests as they engaged in science activities. The porches also served as gathering places for whole group discussions, questions, and directions. Looking at the teachers sitting casually under the oak tree as they waited for Marilyn to wrap up her discussion of how the system worked together, one might think it was a group of friends having a picnic. This was the atmosphere of the first week of the course.

During her questioning of the teachers about the activities they had completed (a census of the compost, a census of the pond, and a census of the woods surrounding Marilyn's home), Marilyn asked how doing the science themselves made them feel about doing the science with kids in their classroom. She also asked what it was like to do the science camp for a second time. Joyce was an original member of the science committee, had piloted the program from the beginning of the grant, and had participated in the camp and class last summer. She replied that it was easier to do the camp this year as she knew that it was "ok, whatever she came up with was ok to try." There was not always a right way to do things or a right answer to the questions posed. She also said that the more that she did the science herself, the more that she felt confident about trying it in her classroom, that it was more interesting.

Mary said that not all kids learn best in an undirected approach and some kids need to have direct instruction to know what to do. She felt that there needed to be a balance of approaches—this is what she has adopted in her own classroom, combining much of the new hands on activities with the former book oriented approach where objectives and information is directly laid out. Karen, who had taught the units in her classroom this past year and participated in grade level planning meetings, replied to Mary's comment, "I think that the more that kids do this kind of learning and activities in the younger grades, it will be easier for them to understand how they are to take more of the responsibility for their learning. They will learn how to learn in this way."

Later that afternoon when class had ended, two of the teachers, Marilyn, her husband, my husband, my daughter and I walked down to the river bottom and through a part of the woods. I talked to Karen. She told me again that she really liked this new science program, but reiterated an earlier conversation. Hands-on learning takes time and kids need time to think through the processes. She worries that she is not taking the time to do it right. Because she feels pressure to make sure that students get all the information—"there isn't time for kids to wonder, they need to learn!"

NOTES

1. Wisconsin Fast Plants are plants that have been developed to go through the entire life cycle of a plant in a 45-day period. They grow leaves and flowers and when they are pollinated produce seed pods which can be used to start the process again.
2. I will explore the issues of imposing the changes and ownership of the idea of change in Chapter 5.

CHAPTER 3

RELATIONSHIPS

MAKING SPACE FOR REFORM/CHANGE OR
TAKING SPACE FROM REFORM/CHANGE

I believe that what I saw happen and what I experienced in the Balmoral
school district as the elementary teachers worked through the changing
science curriculum differs from the traditional way that change is perceived to occur within schools and school systems. As I have said before,
much that has been written about school change has been about what
structural entities are necessary to gain teachers' support in reform
efforts—what administrators and educational leaders should do to promote change. In my experience working with teachers in the Balmoral
schools, I believe that change is a personal process and that teachers must
believe in the reform efforts to make the changes a part of their own
teaching and learning. In other words, the reform is situated in their individual interpretations of the ideas. Not only did teachers find individual
ways to make the changes work for them, to make the changes under-
standable to them, and to find the ways that the changes fit with their own
ideas, I also saw that relationships played a large role in how teachers created their own reality of the changes in their own classrooms. When I say
relationships, I mean relationships between teachers, between teachers
and the curriculum, between teachers and children and between teachers
and administrators. By examining these relationships, the importance of
personal relationships to impact change can be seen. Setting up structural
supports to facilitate change as well as supporting intrinsic motivation for

Teachers and the Reform of Elementary Science, 51–69
Copyright © 2004 by Information Age Publishing
All rights of reproduction in any form reserved.

change are both important factors in the process of improving learning, teaching, and school and relationships with colleagues, with the curriculum and with the change process itself contribute both positively to promote change and negatively to work against reform efforts. This chapter will explore the ideas of relationships and their impact on the process of curricular and pedagogical change.

PROTECTING A COLLABORATIVE RELATIONSHIP

In an earlier chapter, I told the story of Gail's excitement for the soil project that she was doing and her eagerness to share it with me. Gail showed me what she was doing in her classroom, shared her student's work with me, and described her teaching experience to me, but she would not share these stories of success with such excitement to her partner teacher, as their enthusiasm for the projects were not equal. She told me that it was better for her just to stay positive but not go overboard. After the two teachers piloted the unit, I sat down with them one day after school to discuss their thoughts about the unit.

> **Heidi:** Now that you have gone through the full unit on Soils, what would you tell the other second grade teachers who are getting ready teach it?
>
> **Gail:** Definitely allow a full hour for teaching.
>
> **Jan:** You need preparation time. It is helpful to schedule the science if you have some free time before and after for clean up.
>
> **Gail:** You can't trade classes and share the teaching load with this soils unit.
>
> **Jan:** My kids missed the trading part.[1]
>
> **Gail:** But there is to much follow up and the lessons all build on each other so you really need to teach the next lesson to the class you taught before.
>
> **Jan:** You went through the whole book. Do you feel that we need every lesson or is there a spot we could stop? And maybe go into the planting rather than finish up the entire unit? I didn't do the whole thing.
>
> **Gail:** The only thing that we did was the planting in the test tubes where the kids could see the root systems. We identified the local soil and that was really a unit evaluation.
>
> **Jan:** Did you really need to do the root thing?

Gail: I think they could see how the different soil effected the growth of the plants and their roots.

Jan: I did have two parents comment on how much their kids liked the science. Maybe all that struggle was worth it.

COLLABORATING WITH EACH OTHER

"Female work relationships are friendships in which women help each other to belong to themselves." Several years ago a coworker gave me a card on which she had written the above quote. I believe that the ideas stated in that short quote say a great deal about what is possible when teachers work together in a collaborative manner. When teachers work together to support one another in their teaching efforts, in trying new ideas, and in talking about their practice, they gain a certain strength and confidence in the ways they work with each other, their students, and their curriculum. When I first began this research project, I thought the idea of teachers working together would be the main emphasis of the research. In my own teaching, I had always found and worked with other colleagues with whose support we worked to make changes together, motivate each other, and share in reflecting and planning. This had been a part of teaching that I really enjoyed and I felt that giving teachers time to try things out, to talk about those experiences, to plan and make decisions together set up an environment where teachers would certainly work together. As I worked with the teachers, I found that although teachers did take time to talk to each other and to plan with each other when we (Marilyn or myself) carved out time for this to happen, I found that teachers did not always motivate each other to take risks or to change. In some cases the relationships between teachers promoted change as they worked together and saw what was happening in other classroom, but in other cases the relationships between teachers and with the curriculum kept teachers from making as many changes as they might have made if they were not involved in the relationship with their colleagues.

Researchers need to be aware of the realities of trying to construct collaborative projects within public school settings with public school teachers. Clift, Veal, Holland, Johnson, and McCarthy (1995) discuss the context and culture of some schools using a wartime definition of collaboration as a metaphor.

> In wartime, the term collaboration often has been synonymous with treason. Perhaps some of us carry this definition in our heads as we protect our patents, lesson plans, perfectly written paragraphs, and other secrets from those who would steal them for their own profit.... The way we structure our

professional work lives makes collaboration very difficult. (Clift et al., 1995, p. 136)

In this project, the metaphor of soldiers in war could also apply. Teachers came to this project with relationships intact, collaborations that they had created over time working together. Collaboration occurred in many instances and out of conversations in these structured times came many of the decisions about the direction of the curriculum, future learning, or planning sessions. Teachers made decisions about topics, supplies, materials, resources, and also shared questions and concerns as they made these decisions. Teachers also collaborated in times that were not structured by the science teaching (their own planning time, lunch, after school, and in passing between classes). In the following example, two teachers who had worked together for over 10 years planning their teaching, sharing ideas and materials, and supporting one another felt a very strong allegiance to keeping their sense of togetherness. In a sense they protected each other and their relationship throughout the implementation of the new science curriculum, much like soldiers might protect each other in battle. I visited one of their classrooms after school and the teacher, Gail, was very excited about the way things were going. Her students were really enjoying the activities, she felt they were observing and reporting well, and she was also enjoying the inquiry learning. "I know that Jan is not having such a good experience and I am hesitant to push it. I don't want to 'grand-stand.'" Gail was struggling with her successes with the new curriculum because she did not want to jeopardize her collaborative relationship with Jan. When many people are working together and the outcomes are not positive for all, the relationship may become more important than the project.

> Taking responsibility for a dream of educational change that includes collaboration across institutions means, for us, that change is not something that one group prescribes and another enacts. Rather, change is a result of collaboration among people who see themselves as critical friends and who care passionately about another's well-being. In such collaborations, interventions are not imposed by reformers, but evolve through supportive, reflective analyses on data-based information relating practices and perceptions to procedures and goals. (Clift et al., 1995, p. 150)

In this case, valuing the relationship shaped changes in pedagogy and curriculum.

Gail continued to try out new ideas and decided on her own to implement more of the lessons than her teaching partner, another second grade teacher. She did this because she collaborated with Jan on much of their teaching ideas and science was only a part of that collaboration. Gail knew that Jan was not as happy with the science changes and to her it was important not to stray too far from the collaborative relationship that they had worked out for the past 10 years. This is more of their conversation and reflection about a unit.

> **Gail:** The kids were excited and they did look forward to it. They did watch—whether it was sand settling or whatever. They were curious.
>
> **Jan:** I felt overwhelmed with all the supplies and then having to monitor behavior. Next time I'm going to be able to see what I need to address beforehand.
>
> **Gail:** Like the magnifying glasses. We need to have them out before we want them to look at the soils. They could read the newspaper with them or something.
>
> **Jan:** Yes, like I do with the rulers at the beginning of the year. Flip them around, do all those things so its not a novelty anymore. I did try to write some things that I need to change in my book.
>
> **Heidi:** What would make it easier next time? Is it one of the units you will keep for the second grade curriculum?
>
> **Jan:** I liked it.
>
> **Gail:** I think so. I think it will get easier. I'm not sure I will do it all. I'll make that judgment next year after I do it again. It was hard getting it ready, getting it distributed in an orderly fashion, keeping on task, and then getting a response—verbally and then getting them to write it down. Some of our teaching is not geared to this kind of activity. We are used to having the kids look back on the paper to find the answers. We usually brainstormed our observations together and then they chose some to put on their papers.

What I think is interesting about this conversation is that the two teachers take over the questioning of each other and sharing of ideas. I asked a few questions, but the conversation took turns that the teachers directed. I do not know if the teachers would have exchanged their ideas without a formal meeting, but I think the conversation does show the importance of carving out spaces for teachers to exchange their thoughts and reflections about what they are doing or planning to do in their classrooms. I believe that this also shows the power that colleagues have upon each other.

Gail valued her relationship with Jan and knew what she wanted to do to keep things comfortable, for herself in her classroom and also in her working relationships with her colleagues. She wanted and needed the support of her teaching partner, had enjoyed a long relationship of sharing ideas, supplies, and support and wanted to continue the positive aspects of this relationship that the two teachers had fostered. Noddings (1992) gives an alternative approach to education that includes ideas of caring for others. In her vision of female friendship, Raymond (1986, p. 218) defines one aspect of female friendship as thoughtfulness. "*[T]houghtfulness* is characterized on one hand by ability to reason and on the other by considerateness and caring." This is what Gail is exhibiting as she tries to balance her own ideas about what she wants to do in her own classroom with the relationship that she has with Jan. She wants to continue to work together (considerateness and caring for Jan's opinions and feelings about the changes) and also to enjoy the experiences she is having with the changes (thinking/reason).

IS WHAT WE ARE DOING CONSISTENT WITH WHAT WE BELIEVE?

Rob and Mary were of the first group of teachers to invite me into their classrooms. Both were sixth grade teachers who taught at least two sections of science during each school day. For this reason, and because of their own interest in science, they had both been active in the initiation of the new science curriculum and on the science committee. Rob is a young teacher, entering his third year of teaching and Mary had been teaching for about 10 years. They both live in the district and are involved in the community. Rob's wife also teaches for the district. Mary grew up in the town and has two children enrolled in the Balmoral schools. Each of the teachers seemed eager in the planning sessions to work through the new curriculum, add in ideas from their existing curriculum, and to involve writing and reading in the science activities.

The first unit that their two classes would pilot was a unit on plants. In their study, students would experiment with the variables that effect plant growth: things like amounts of light, amounts of fertilizer, spacing of plants. The students in this study would design their own experiments and make individual and group conclusions based on the growth of their Wisconsin Fast Plants over the 45-day growing period. Before the study began, the two teachers invited me to help them do an inventory of the supplies and make sure that they understood what each of the items would be used for. Organization was an important factor for Mary as she began a new teaching experience. She told me that she just wanted to know what she was "getting into" before she began. After getting to know her over the following two years, visiting her classroom and talking together, I could see that her style of teaching needed this straightforward control over the supplies and set up. Mary was very direct in her easy-going manner with the kids and wanted them to understand her expectations as they worked through the learning experiments. She gave very direct instructions for completion of some creative projects that she had designed to incorporate other subject matter into science and also to bring together some of the ideas her class had been studying. One example was a "bee poster." The directions and explanation of the project stated:

> Your poster must contain the following:
> 1. Large drawing of a bee = 20 pts.
> 2. Major body parts must be labeled (tongue, jaws, head, antennae, simple eyes, compound eyes, thorax, front legs, middle legs, back legs, abdomen, fore wing, hind wing, pollen basket, sting) = 15 pts.
> 3. Describe five of the body parts = 10 pts.
> 4. 15 facts about bees = 45 pts.
> 5. You must use at least two resources. Include the bibliographic information for each source = 10 pts.

I do not give this example to discuss the merits of the learning of a project of this type, but I do want to note that kids in Mary's class were completely absorbed in reading the bee books she had accumulated from the local and school libraries. I give this example to show how the teacher incorporated her own needs into the curriculum she designed. Mary needed to have direct expectations outlined for her students, even when her goal was to have the students read about and find their own interesting ideas and questions about bees and their relationship to the plants they were growing. I believe that because her own personality and needs were embedded in the assignment, she was able to create an environment where she felt comfortable teaching and her kids felt comfortable learning. What happens when the ideas and beliefs of teaching partners do not match up?

Rob's classroom and teaching became a contrast to Mary's teaching even though they were working from the same curriculum and had even planned some of the teaching ideas together. Rob was very happy to go along with these discussions, planning, and preparations. He was also happy to incorporate the projects that Mary had designed. It became quite clear to me that he had a different agenda that became a part of his teaching and one that he was very open about expressing. An example of his beliefs about teaching science and his open expression of these beliefs became evident during the teacher course part of the summer science camp. Part of the course requirement was a completion of a nature journal. In this inquiry assignment, the teachers chose an aspect of nature that they would observe closely for a week. They would express their careful observations through writing and art activities (Chancer & Rester-Zodrow, 1997). The teachers were asked to share their journals with us, telling us what they thought about the assignment, how they felt it contributed to their learning of science or science teaching, and either read or show us at least one of their activities. Although most of the teachers were modest in talking about their own work, it was evident by the way that they put their work together and the quality of the writing and art, that they were mostly proud of the finished products, their level of interest in their topic, and the learning and questions that their observations had produced. We felt that it was an example of how doing a learning activity creates a relationship with the learning that just talking about or reading about cannot do. When Rob read his poem to our group of 15 sitting in a circle in the library of the school, everyone seemed to be engaged and listened politely enjoying the creativity of the rhymes. The type of poem that Rob based his writing on was a fact-based poem described in our text as a poem intended to find the answers in scientific study by "looking at the moon through the eyes of a scientist" (Chancer & Rester-Zodrow, 1997, p. 89).

If You Were the Moon how Old Would You Be?

If you were the Moon, how old would you be?
Not all scientists agree, so let the evidence speak.
Unfortunately, the answer has been one-sided,
How old is it really? Let's let the evidence guide us.
Four and a half billion years is what were often told,
But there are many reasons to believe it's not nearly that old.
Radioactive dating is the process normally used,
That gives these incredibly old ages, but don't be confused.
There are many problems with this method of dating,
Let me give you an example of what I am saying.
There is a volcano that lies many miles away,
On the north island of New Zealand where in the 1950's there came a day,
When it erupted and left lava that hardened real soon,
Becoming igneous rock, the same kind they found on the Moon.
A sample was sent to be dated this way,
And you won't believe the results that they got on that day.
3 1/2 million years old is what they reported,
A gigantic mistake which must be discarded.
People saw these rocks form less than 50 years ago,
A very telling fact which just goes to show,
You cannot always trust what scientists say about the past,
And with that I come to my conclusion at last.
Always study the evidence and there is so much more that will show,
That the Creator made the Moon around 6,000 years ago.

When Rob read the last line of the poem, there was a pregnant pause before the group clapped as we had been doing as each teacher completed his or her sharing. There was definitely an indecision on how to react to the way that Rob was interpreting the science of his inquiry, one that did not seem to fit with the way that the other teachers saw religion and science working together in this public school system. I think there was also some shock in the boldness of Rob reading his ideas like this in such an open forum. I had seen him do this in his classroom in a discussion about a video. The video was about pollination of various plants around the world. It showed the intricate ways that the plants were structured to work with their environment to ensure pollination. He built a discussion around one idea. "Do you see a master plan at work here? These are not random actions. These plants have been *created* with a plan in mind."

This describes and shows a tension that exists when teachers have the freedom to mold the curriculum to fit their own beliefs and ideas about learning. How is this balance checked? Are standardized tests the way to keep teachers philosophies in check and is this the way that we want an open and thinking society to teach its children? What happens when a teacher's philosophy about teaching or what constitutes science does not agree with his or her teaching partners?

> Many schools that advocate strong professional communities boast mutual shared obligations and commitments. But these are often slogans such as "acceptance of all children" or a "desire to serve ideals." Whose ideals? What do these teachers believe in? What kind of world do they strive for? (Westheimer, 1998, p. 139)

I asked Mary about collaborating with Rob one day after Rob, she, and I had brainstormed some project ideas for their plant unit.

Heidi: Does it help to work with another teacher in planning and evaluating the unit?

Mary: I like working with another teacher when it is a reciprocal relationship, when both people are contributing. It is hard to work together when you have differing beliefs about what science is.

Heidi: I wondered about that.

Mary: We don't work together as much as we probably could.

COLLABORATING TOWARD CHANGE

For most of the teachers, the relationships that they shared with their grade level partners and with other teachers in their building and district, the spaces set up for collaboration were a natural continuation of the relationships that the teachers already shared. Much like Jan and Gail, and even Rob and Mary, the teachers shared some ideas, reflections, and supplies in working through common teaching experiences. For most of the groups who worked together to make decisions about curriculum, to plan units and lessons, and to reflect on their teaching experiences the spaces carved out for sharing of ideas created an atmosphere that built on their relationships and past experiences to continue working together in a similar manner. After almost every meeting, the teachers commented on how nice it was to have time and to make time to sit down and talk about their teaching experiences. On an evaluation form that the district curriculum coordinator sent out during the second year of working through the new science curriculum and pedagogy, teachers responded very favorably to a question about the planning sessions. The question asked, "What did you find most favorable about the sessions?"

> Talking with other teachers about their units. I would like to have more time to spend discussing successes and lessons that need refining.

> I appreciate the fact that all grade levels had an opportunity to be together and share ideas. It was helpful to hear about lessons that have been successful as well as problems that might have occurred.

> Being with other grade level teachers.

> Sharing ideas with other teachers in the same grade level.

> Sharing with the other teachers! Problem solving and troubleshooting helps us maintain focus on the goals of the units.

> The open communication between all members and the team brain-storming were very valuable.

> Just having the time to get together and talk and share ideas.

> Planning together with grade-level and having a block of planning and work time.

These comments paralleled what the teachers told me when I asked them if they liked taking the time to have conversations about the changes. It is evident that the teachers enjoyed spending time together, time that they did not take otherwise to meet together, and talking about the specifics of the changes that the new science program had brought to their classrooms.

In one of her essays, Anna Quinlan (1988, p. 45) describes time that she spent with a good friend:

> Neither felt the need to be sociable, or polite: more than once, we picked up our respective books and started to read at opposite ends of the couch. Most of the time we talked and talked, not in a linear way, but as though we were digging for buried treasure. Why did you feel that way? And what did you say then? What are you going to do about that? How long did that go on? It was an extended version of the ladies' lunches in which we bring our psyches out of from inside our purses, lay them on the table, and fold them up again after coffee.

This description is an appropriate metaphor for most of the grade level meetings that Marilyn and I shared with the teachers. The conversations were not linear; the teachers wanted to know details of the way things worked in each other' classrooms. The topics moved from the personal (of people who have worked together and known each other for many years) to memories of other curriculum used, to kids and families they knew, and back to topics of curricular change. They made themselves vulnerable by sharing failures, successes, and questions and concerns that they had. We ate lunches together and then we all went on our way, folding up our purses full of the ideas we had shared and went back to our jobs of teaching and learning.

This is an example conversation from a third grade meeting. It is very typical of the kinds of exchanges that took place when teachers shared their experiences. This meeting was held in the fall of the second year of the project. Jennie is telling the other two teachers, David and Joyce, about her experiences with a unit on plants. This particular discussion centers around using freeze-dried bees to pollinate the plants.[2]

Jennie: Make sure that you glue the bees, bottom side up. Otherwise their heads break off and I wanted the kids to see the legs and the bodies and the bottoms all get the pollen off the plants. So then we just buzzed around the table and pollinated the plants.

Heidi: Were the bees worthwhile? You could use a q-tip, but not quite as interesting.

Jennie: Oh, yes, the kids loved looking at them. We got out those magnifying glasses that we have from the rock unit. Bob [her principal] got those for us. So I just have a set that I keep in the classroom. We used them all the time—looking at the plants, the bees, looking for the pollen. They are great.

Joyce: We need those. There is a set in the rock unit, but not for each of us to have in our own room. Maybe the PTA could buy them.

David comes back to the meeting from checking on his substitute.

Joyce: We're talking about having a set of those magnifying glasses with the lights for our own classrooms.
Jennie: I really miss having Joan in my room. You know Joan.
Joyce: Yeah she took over for Paula …
Jennie: She just adopted a baby and is doing great.
Joyce: Oh …
Jennie: But we used to really team teach—she was so good and we'd just throw everything, whatever out. It just worked out really well. She helped me figure lots of this out and when the kids were pollinating it was a big help.
David: So to the bees, I just stick it through the top of them …
Jennie: No, I just hot glued them. They want you to look at all the parts and if you stick it to them, they'll break apart.
Joyce: So you did it, not the kids.
Jennie: Yes, and do it bottom up. (Everyone laughs.) But you guys do what you want, I'm just telling you what worked for me.
David: You almost want to see underneath too.
Jennie: Yeah, but you spend time looking at the bee first before you glue them on.
Joyce: So then you went around and glued them on?
Jennie: I did it during my lunch hour.
David: So you're looking at your bee in one lesson and in the next lesson?
Jennie: You pollinate.
Joyce: You really put something on, they really do. You mean you really pollinate or this is just pretend.
Jennie: What do you mean? Yes, you are really pollinating. You take your bee and you go from this flower to this flower to this flower. You don't have to go buzzzz unless you want to Joyce. (She is laughing.)
David: I thought you were just going around the room buzzing and I thought, "Oh god, we're not doing that!" (Everyone is laughing.)
Jennie: Oh no, you are really pollinating and then they can get out their microscope and look at their little bottoms and

see the pollen. (She begins to sing, "Let me tell you about the birds and the bees." We are laughing.)

Heidi: Did you get any questions about that?

David: You know how we pollinate these flowers? They touch bottoms.

Jennie: Well some times it is hard with these third graders. But, no, I didn't say that. I didn't want any phone calls.

David: Well, I had Jack Johnson, and Larry White, and John Ruggle one year in the same group and we got into X and Y chromosomes in science. We were talking about the planets or something. I don't know where that came from, and I kind of went off too much I think. (They laugh.)

Jennie: Then the workers bite off the drone's wings and unceremoniously throw them out in the cold. That's what it says here. So I got out the encyclopedia and let the kids look up about bees. They were interested after looking at them. Well, when a queen bee dies off, how do they get a new queen bee? So we looked that up. Kids were reading all about that.

David: Is there another queen bee that's born?

Jennie: Well, I'm going to let you find out for yourself. Ask Jeeves. (She is referring to a joke we laughed at earlier. We laugh again.) But that is something that they ask you and now that is something you can look up. My lips are sealed.

Heidi: See, you're not going to be bored.

Jennie: No, you're not going to be bored, honey. You're going to be learning all kinds of things.

David: Well, I learned about rocks last year.

This conversation may seem on the surface to be simply three teachers figuring out how to glue a bee on a stick and use it to pollinate flowers. By examining the exchanges carefully there is a genuine comfort level. Here are three teachers laughing together, exchanging ideas about what worked and what did not work, asking questions, and admitting that they do not know all the scientific facts. They make themselves vulnerable by asking questions. There is a story within this conversation about the excitement of learning how to teach something new and how to learn along with the students. Although this third grade team was not always in agreement about the ways that science should be taught in the classroom and did not always feel that they were preparing their students for the state tests, these teachers did use their relationships with one another to learn about the curriculum, the pedagogy, and how best to make it work for each of them individually.

PROCESS AND PRODUCT IN TEACHING AND LEARNING: RELATIONSHIPS WITH THE CHILDREN AND RELATIONSHIPS WITH THE CURRICULUM

It is not only teachers' relationships with each other that impacts the changes made in classrooms, but also a teacher's relationship with the curriculum and the children. During the first summer science camp, Margery Osborne and I cotaught the kindergarten class. During our two weeks with the 18 six-year-old students, we studied a garden, learning to look closely at the colors, textures, and design of the plants and garden. For a part of each morning, usually after a visit to the garden, we set up several centers in the classroom. The centers had to do with some aspect of the garden and interests that the children had in the garden. One of the activities was using magnets that Margery had made from seed catalogue pictures. They were beautiful photographs of flowers in every color, laminated and stuck to business card sized magnets. The students in our kindergarten class loved the magnets that Margery had made. They created lovely designs of matching colors—a pink garden, a lavender garden, an all green garden. They worked with partners, in groups, or alone on these projects sticking the magnets to the steel lockers in patterns and designs.

When Margery began making the magnets during our preparation time before the kids arrived, I thought "oh, that's a good idea. The kids can design gardens and see similarities and differences between the plants, their colors and their textures." But, I never dreamed that the kids would create such an elaborate system of playing with the magnets. As the two-week class continued and we continued to give the children choices of activities during the center time, the magnets became a culture of their own. The kindergartners made up an interesting game with the magnets, sort of a cross between the card games "go fish" and "war." They made up the rules and seemed to understand each other when they played. There were no fights about who was taking all the cards. The kids gathered around the table, passed out the magnets, and started to play. I became fascinated with watching them play this game. They had taken a topic of study and objects that represented this topic of study (the garden and the flower magnets) and constructed a game that was both familiar to them and new at the same time. They were interested in the pictures of flowers, obviously looking at them in ways to distinguish which was a "winner" in the game, but it certainly was not the way the I would have pictured them finding similarities and differences. They had created a much more complex understanding of these flowers and their relation to one another in order to make these magnets with flowers on them something that they could relate to. What kind of excitement would have been generated if Margery or I had simply told them to find all the flowers that have small petals or are similar in color? The goals would have been the same, but as it happened, the students' process of learning became an important part of their learning.

TENSIONS OF TEACHING: IMPLICIT AND EXPLICIT SCIENCE

I write these stories about my own teaching experiences with the project because I think they give an interesting viewpoint to some of the issues that I saw the teachers working through. I began to find my own sort of tension with the ideas of "was I teaching enough science" to satisfy the parents, the other teachers, the children during the second summer science camp. This was the last summer that we were involved in the summer science camp and the teacher in-service that paralleled the camp.

The second summer of the camp Margery and I used cooking as the theme for our science class. We decided on this theme much earlier in the year and were both excited about the topic of cooking. During our planning time, we set up the space in the classroom to give the students in our second grade class every opportunity to take control of their learning. We set out the tools and equipment for cooking (measuring cups and spoons, bowls of all sizes, spoons, graters, etc.), books for cooking (both directed towards children and directed toward adult readers), and sources of heat for the cooking itself (hotplates, microwave, electric skillets). We would also create a space for the ingredients needed. Our beginning idea was to give the children some direction in creating a group menu for the day and also to give the students choice and freedom for making decisions about what they would cook and how they would create their recipes. We wanted the act of cooking, the creation of the recipe, the playing with the ingredients to be an empowering experience for the students. We wanted them to see that they had the power to make the decisions about their learning— what worked, what did not, how the recipes became food to eat, what changes they could make in the recipes to make them better, and also how to negotiate these ideas with their cooking groups. In talking about how we thought the two-week camp would progress, it seemed clear that cooking embodied the ideas of scientific thought and process and fit in very well with the inquiry teaching that the other teachers were trying out as well.

Both Margery and I felt that the topic of cooking and the act of cooking implicitly held many science topics and processes. As I typed our introductory letter to the parents, I felt the need to make these concepts and processes more explicit. I felt a need to make sure that we were clearly "doing science." I wrote to the parents, "Through cooking, we will explore concepts of measurements, changes in state and matter, and effects of heat on changes of state and matter. We will be using science skills/processes including observing, measuring, predicting, communicating, hypothesizing, and experimenting." But, as the children became more involved in their own cooking creations, actively participating in making decisions about what and how to cook, and negotiating with their groups the explicit ideas of "science" became less important to me. As I became less of a directive teacher and the students took increasingly more control of their learning, I worried less and less about making the scientific point—I could see the students using the science as they experimented with the cooking. Their relationship with the summer science camp curriculum changed my own relationship with the curriculum. Although I continued to feel some of the tension of "was I teaching enough 'science,'" this feeling was not at the forefront in deciding the structure of the class sessions. At the beginning of the two-week session, I asked Margery to carve out a space for the "teaching of science concepts." The following is a discussion about what happened when we opened a refrigerated can of crescent rolls. The purpose of this activity was to explore the kids' ideas about what made the dough in a refrigerated can of dough expand and pop through its packaging. We tried to relate that expansion of the dough (the reaction that is continually taking place in the dough) to a chemical reaction that they could see and describe. Margery is demonstrating that reaction.

Margery:	This reaction, right now, is the same reaction that is happening all the time even though its in the can. When you open it up, it pops and gets big just like it does in the oven.
Heidi:	It has room to get big.
Margery:	Now, what I'm going to do is put some vinegar in the bottle. You don't need very much.
Heidi:	Now she's putting in the baking soda.

Kids are talking about how this is exactly what they did in their classroom.

Lauren:	It's going to make a very big balloon.
Margery:	Now I'm putting in the baking soda. That's all the gas and you can see all the bubbles in here (she points to the reaction taking place in the plastic soda bottle) and

that's what happens in the crescent rolls. And also in pancakes and in cakes and all those other things.

Heidi: Remember how you said that our pancakes were kind of flat? Did we put any baking soda in our pancakes? What would happen if we put some in?

I'm trying to connect this science to the cooking we did yesterday. The kids do not respond as they excitedly watch the balloon expand.

Margery: What's going on here? This is a special kind of air here. It is not the kind of air that we breathe. What is it?

Jake: It is the kind of air that comes out of you when you breathe out.

Margery: That's right. How do you know all that?

Jake: (He laughs.) Because I watch Arthur.[3]

At the end of the morning as we group together to talk about what we did that day, Margery asks the kids what we learned about. She tells them that we learned about chemical reactions, making sure to use a "scientific term" for my benefit and for the parents as well. I knew the kids were learning about science as they created their cakes, changing ingredients and amounts as they saw fit. I knew that they were learning to put together procedures and negotiate with their learning groups the ways that their cooking experiments would turn out. I knew that they were making observations, making decisions, and making conclusions based on their cooking experiences. I knew that these were all sound scientific processes and concepts, but I still felt that unease. Was it enough explicit science for the parents, for the other teachers, and did the kids need to know what explicitly was science? Our making sure that the students went home knowing the name and talking about "chemical reactions" parallels that feeling that the teachers in the district have when they want the children in their classes to perform well on the state and district tests. The teachers liked the experiments generally, liked the excitement that the kids had toward learning science, but they questioned whether that was enough. Would the kids know enough to show the community that they were learning as well as liking learning?

CONCLUDING NOTES

I have tried in this chapter to show that relationships play an important role in shaping the ways that change occurs in classrooms. The relationships between teachers and their colleagues, between teachers and the curriculum, and between teachers and their students impact the ways that the changing curriculum was enacted in the classroom. In the example of Gail and her soil unit, her relationship with her fellow teacher inhibited her own enthusiasm for the changing curriculum and pedagogy. Mary felt that her own philosophy about science differed so much from her teaching partner that it made it very difficult to plan and work together on the changing curriculum. She felt it was just easier to work on her own and let Rob use her ideas if he wanted. In the case of my own teaching, I felt the same type of tensions that the teachers expressed to me many times over—the wonder of watching the children be engaged in their own learning, but also wondering if I was providing the students with enough "science." This dynamic relationship with the curriculum shaped the ways that I planned and impacted the science lessons and units in my own teaching. These relationships, those with other people involved in the changes, those with the changing curriculum itself, and the relationships that unfolded as the children interacted with their own learning created the unique and individual ways that the science curriculum evolved in each different classroom. I think that these stories show that change is a personal process and how teachers find ways to make the changes fit their own ideas. Finding ways to make the changes fit into their own ideas (enacted in the lesson that they teach and how they teach them in their individual classrooms) is a process where they negotiate through the relationships that they have with other teachers, with the curriculum and pedagogy, with the community. It is the ways that they interpret these relationships that reflects their values and the personal decisions and choices that they make about enacting the curricular changes. These choices reflect more than just subject matter considerations, but also, from these stories, the ways that subject matter is approached (in the case of Mary and Rob and also in my own experience of defining science teaching) the ways that colleagues are included in celebrations and tensions of change (in the case of Gail and Jan and also in the third grade team supporting one another).

How can a school district's educational leadership factor in the multitude of ways that these relationships will impact one another and the reform efforts? Relationships cannot be legislated by a state test or by standards, they cannot be enforced by providing planning time and placement of classroom to encourage that teachers work together, nor can they be forced by having teachers experience the inquiry method themselves. But, I do believe that by providing spaces for the teachers to reflect on the ways that some of these ideas impact their own teaching, teachers began to explore and examine why they did certain things certain ways in their classrooms. This is an excerpt from what one teacher wrote in her journal at the end of the second summer science camp. From her statements, her values and what influences the personal decisions she makes about implementing reform are better understood.

> I have high expectations for my classroom and for myself—to provide a learning atmosphere where there is enough structure so that the students know what is expected of them and enough freedom to feel comfortable and accepted. It is within this framework that I have been trying to adjust my teaching to provide hands-on exploring and learning while at the same time feeling confident that the children are achieving at a level expected by my school. After two years of teaching science this way [hands-on, inquiry approach] I feel that I have made progress toward this goal. I have put in a lot of time and energy studying the units and reading the manuals and now it is getting easier. It has also gotten easier for the students because they have been exposed to this approach for two years as well. I am still concerned about assessment. I feel that it is still trial and error on my part, but I will keep trying.

As this teacher continues to "try" to make the changes work for her, the evolving relationships that she has with the curriculum, with the students, and with the larger community of her school will impact her personal and on-going negotiations.

NOTES

1. The two teachers had traded classes for science twice a week before switching to the new curriculum. Each teacher taught the same lesson twice, once to her own class and once to her partner's class. There are two other second grade teachers who had a similar system worked out.
2. In this third grade unit, which the sixth grade unit described earlier builds on, the students learn the life cycle and parts of a plant. Part of the cycle is pollination. The students manually pollinate their Wisconsin Fast Plants with dried bees glued to a stick, simulating what happens in a natural environment.
3. "Arthur" is an animated children's show on PBS which is based on books by Mark Brown.

CHAPTER 4

STRUCTURAL SUPPORTS

A STORY ABOUT "STUFF"

The teachers both love Marilyn for her stories and hate Marilyn for her stories. It is not really that they hate her, but they hate the fact that her story-telling takes up their planning time—time that they would rather be talking about the task at hand, making progress toward their goal, checking this task off of their list. But the stories also endear Marilyn to them, they show the teachers that Marilyn is a teacher, has much experience, is a part of their community, and show the teachers a personal side of Marilyn—her stories tell about her home, her hobbies, her feelings, and her family. They are stories that make connections to the teachers, for they share in her teaching experiences, family life, hobbies, and the community. The stories in many ways built bridges between people, for they showed the ways that people view things and think about things, what they have in common and the kinds of ideas that they believe in.

This particular conversation contains a story that Marilyn told at several of our grade-level meetings that were held during the summer before beginning the second year implementing the new science units. In these meetings the teachers were talking through the units they had chosen to teach in the coming school year. Then they compiled lists of the supplies and materials needed to teach the units. As it is with many teachers, the teachers always began by trying to "get by." What was the least amount of items they could order? Which were the least expensive? What could they

---

Teachers and the Reform of Elementary Science, 71–87
Copyright © 2004 by Information Age Publishing
All rights of reproduction in any form reserved.

contribute from their own collections of teaching materials? What could be substituted for the materials needed?

Marilyn: You are asked to spend your own five dollars here and five dollars there—you're nickeled and dimed to death. You should be spending your time and energy on classroom teaching. The other is the community's problem.

Jennie: I'm just trying to find what I need.

Marilyn: I know you are. We all are.

Heidi: She's not trying to make us feel guilty.

Marilyn: I'm not trying to make you feel bad. I'm trying to make you feel like you don't have to do this anymore. For science anyway …

David: Well, it is such a relief off of my shoulders just to even know that there is someone that is going to be there to do all that and all I have to do is get the kit and I know it is going to be ready.

Marilyn: That's right.

Jennie: Absolutely.

David: You don't know how much stress that relieves, because you are always worried about starting and not having something. I mean how many times have you been ready to do a lesson and realize …

Heidi: That you forgot to stop at the store and get the whatever …

Marilyn: And you pay for it out of you own pocket nine out of 10 times because it's easier.

David: Yeah …

Marilyn: Well, its no wonder, then, that we don't teach a lot of hands-on activity based science in the classroom then. To me it is the profession's responsibility to understand that and take care of that problem. It is not yours and yours and yours and mine to take care of that "stuff."

Jennie: It's hard sometimes to get a purchase order and to get it approved ahead of time. And then if you do buy something, they say, "Well, we're not paying for that."

Marilyn: And I understand why they have to do that. If you have 100 people out there who are arbitrarily buying things that they decide that they want for their classrooms, you have control and knowing how much and what money is being spent. So that's why I think, it behooves us to get this thing organized and know it is going to cost this much to do this kind of teaching and then support it.

> And we are supporting it by not buying a textbook. When you take $35 per kid, that is thousands of dollars. You wouldn't be responsible to buy a textbook for every kid in your class. It is the school district's, the community's responsibility to get you the things you need to teach— but it is our responsibility to organize it and set it up in such a way that it is efficient.

Marilyn continues with the story that she told at several of the grade level meetings.

> I can remember working along time ago, you know, and we were cleaning up at the end of the year and another teacher had all of her papers and files organized in boxes. She had covered them in contact paper. While we were working one day, she said to me, "What other business in this town does not provide enough file cabinets for their workers? Nobody else." And I said you are right. And we are doing the community's work and the their kids' work and I just think sometimes we put ourselves in this position, we let ourselves just get by.

David: Yeah, I got all my filing cabinets at garage sales. (He is chuckling.)

Marilyn: Its not your job to have to get the things you need to teach. Your job is to think about the kids and do the best you can for them and that's why you go to garage sales because otherwise you wouldn't have the stuff. So you do it because you want the kids to have them. We are professional and we shouldn't have to beg for necessities. We are not going to act like we can't afford this stuff. We need it. The money in this grant and the purpose of the money in this grant is to buy materials that you need to do a good job of teaching science. We need to approach this with high expectations of the district. What lawyer, what doctor has to provide their stuff? Or go to a garage sale to get the stuff they need to do their job? I think we are doing a very important professional job and the community has to support that. They have to with enough money for the way it ought to be done without sending you out on scavenger hunts. And that is my story.

Marilyn told this story to try to make the teachers think about teaching and how the quality supplies could reflect values and needs to the community. If the teachers expected quality materials and expected that the materials be provided to them and not by them and then used them in effective ways to teach their students, the community would also expect that the district fund those supplies. I found it a particularly empowering story and by the time that she finished telling it and the teachers reflected on the ways that they have always gone above and beyond to gather the materials needed for teaching, they felt empowered by that message. As they accumulated the ideas for the items they would need to teach the units, their attitudes changed. They asked for everything they thought they would need and did not talk about what they could find at garage sales next summer and what they could make with supplies they had in their garages at home. They looked through catalogues, asked Marilyn questions, and made lists of books that they wanted the librarian to order to support their science teaching. Providing the supplies needed to teach hands-on, activity-based science lessons and units may seem like a simple endeavor and one that must take place for science learning to take place in classrooms. Supports like this are the kinds of things that could be provided with financing, but other kinds of supports were also needed to create a system where teachers could understand the changes for themselves and, as Marilyn said, "to concentrate on the teaching in their classrooms."

STRUCTURAL SUPPORTS

As I mentioned in the introductory chapter, much of what has been written about school change and reform efforts has been directed toward administrative and policy-making agendas. Although these agendas do include the teacher in making changes and decisions in schools, the main focus has been on teacher's role in participating in the structured reform effort, not on the personal process of changing curriculum and pedagogy in individual classrooms. Administrators, teachers, and leaders of reform efforts need to focus on this personal aspect of school change and make sure that the structural supports put in place facilitate the idea that teachers need to understand the ideas of change and have opportunities to find ways for the changes to mesh with their own values and understandings about teaching. In this chapter, I will explore the type of structures that created situations where teachers were encouraged to construct, to explore, and to understand the science curricular and pedagogical reform efforts that they were implementing in their classrooms.

When I say structural supports, I mean not only providing the teachers with the concrete items needed to teach the science units, but also concrete times set aside for teachers to talk together, to reflect on their ideas and experiences and to make decisions about teaching and learning that is best for them and their students. I also mean conceptual support for teachers in the form of spaces to take these ideas and decisions and try them out, think them through, and figure out for themselves what works best in their own classrooms. I will argue that these types of structures are necessary, and that they must be balanced with an understanding that reform is a personal process—the two can and need to work together in order for change to occur with individual teachers, their classrooms, and therefore in schools and districts.

Supporting Teachers with Supplies

One of the reasons teachers balk at the idea of teaching science, especially in a hands-on and inquiry method, is that they feel that the supplies, the set-up, and the organization of the supplies is a huge undertaking (Harms & Yager, 1981). They do not feel that they have the time, energy, and resources to give their students consistent and effective inquiry lessons to meet all of the state and district goals. When the district hired a part-time science clerk who would take time and energy to provide the supplies needed in the classrooms, some of the concerns about materials were alleviated. The clerk was responsible for ordering, maintaining, and organizing the supplies and materials. She stocked the tubs[1] and refurbished them when the teachers finished teaching a unit. Having a clerk to take care of gathering and organizing the supplies took that responsibility away from the teachers. This did give them an opportunity to use that energy and time to concentrate on teaching, but it also created some other tensions.

It became interesting to see the ways that this idea of getting the stuff needed to teach began to evolve as teachers began to take ownership of the ideas and also as their expectations changed. In the beginning of this project, the teachers were generally very excited and enthused about the materials that were provided to them in their teaching kits. Joyce wrote in her journal after teaching during the summer science camp for the first time and after her first year of teaching the new science curriculum. She relates the supplies to the pedagogy:

> I have learned that this kind of teaching can be done when we have the materials available to use. When I have done this unit (a study of simple machines) in the past I didn't have any of the materials like pulleys, boards, etc. This summer we had some of these available plus we brought in tools, nails, boards from home to use. We had time to plan ahead and get the supplies we needed. That is so necessary to do this type of teaching.

As the teachers became accustomed to the idea of materials and supplies being provided for their science lessons, some of their expectations changed and they were not always pleased by what was provided, annoyed when materials were left out, or when supplies and materials were not exactly their preference. Their expectations of the district and their own definitions of their job as the teacher had changed. For example, David and I were discussing how the unit on simple machines was going. He immediately told me about problems with some dowel rods in the kit. They were too short and their diameter was too large for the activities he had planned to do. He was able to improvise and had the kids use their pencils instead of a dowel rod and David said it really was not a "big deal, things worked out." What I find interesting is that using the pencils to create a place for a pulley to hang is a very easy way (and perhaps a better way) to adapt the materials to make the activity work for the kids in his class. This is something that David would have done readily before he expected the materials to be provided for him, something that he would have defined as part of his job—to get the materials needed to teach his lessons. As he became more involved in the teaching and the changes in the curriculum and did not have to concern himself with collecting or providing the materials, he felt a loss of control over this part of teaching. This is a give and take that many of the teachers readily gave up, but also noticed when things were not to their specifications.

Alice tried out many of the activities and lessons in the unit about changes during the summer science camp. She took careful notes and compiled a list of additional supplies that she needed to teach many lessons that were extensions beyond the basic curriculum. When she began to teach the unit in the fall, several items were not included in the kit. She was very patient with the clerk as they learned to communicate their needs to each other, and her principal was very supportive in providing money for her to gather some of the supplies. She stated, "I am just having fun teaching these lessons and the kids are so interested in them, it makes it frustrating when you realize you don't have the supplies you need." Again, before Alice gave up the control over finding the supplies she needed, this would not have been something she ever thought about.

Community Conversations as a Structural Support

In the following conversation, fourth grade teachers talk about choosing a topic for study. Part of the reason that the teachers were interested in revamping their science program had to do with the district's scope and sequence. Many of the teachers felt that the students were getting a hit and miss approach to science curriculum as teachers generally followed the book for their grade level, but then added in and left out what they wanted to. By moving to a more process-based teaching and learning approach the topics would not be the focus, but the skills would build from one grade to the next. This was a major change in thinking about what constitutes science teaching and learning. Teachers still were territorial about the topics they chose for their grade levels to teach and because they were only teaching four in-depth units, they wanted very much to make sure that they were making the "right" decision—for them, for their students, and for the district. This conversation highlights some of the types of considerations teachers made as they chose the topics for the units they would teach. Through conversations such as these, during planning sessions guided by Marilyn, teachers talked through their ideas and used each others' thoughts to build confidence in their choices. We met in the library of the grade school a few weeks before school started. As we sat around a small table, we talked about the three units the teachers had already taught and worked to decide what the fourth unit of study the fourth grade would study.

> **Rich:** So we have three of our four—electricity, motion and design, and animal studies.
>
> **Marilyn:** And then a fourth one. Do you know what you want to do or not?
>
> **Rich:** Well, it seems like, maybe we could choose between soils, solar systems, earth forms, sound? Does that sound right?
>
> **Marilyn:** OK, well let's take a look at it this way. Second grade is already doing soils.
>
> **Rich:** Well, then those three: solar systems, earth forms, and sound.
>
> **Sandy:** But there isn't a kit for solar systems.
>
> **Heidi:** Or for earth forms—those are ones that you would totally have to assemble yourselves.
>
> **Marilyn:** There is also land and water.
>
> **Liz:** Which might tie into what you guys already do.
>
> **Sandy:** That was more erosion …
>
> **Rich:** We were least interested in that.
>
> **Liz:** So it didn't tie into your stuff that you already do.
>
> **Marilyn:** There is consideration to be made in relation to that. Electric circuits, motion and design are both physical sciences. Animal studies is a life science. You have no earth studies at this point. If you did sound, it would be another physical study. If you did solar systems, it's kind of an earth study. It would go in that category.
>
> **Heidi:** When you did sound this summer, did you use a kit, or make it up on your own?

Sandy: We just made it up because we didn't have a kit. Did we have the book?

Liz: We had the book so we did some of that and we used some stuff that we got up at Illinois State.

Heidi: Did you like it?

Sandy: Yeah. The kids really liked it, except as she's saying that's three physicals and maybe that's. . .

Liz: We really need an Earth.

Everyone agrees.

Marilyn: So I think either Land and Water or Measuring Time, but that's jumping up a couple of grade levels.

Rich: Time would be earth science?

Marilyn: What makes time?

Rich: Oh, OK. Revolution and rotation.

Liz: Actually, I just read a book about the first clocks in England and how that changed the whole world. I never thought about that.

Marilyn: Interesting isn't it? Bigger change in civilization than almost anything. Even electronics. For one thing, then they could navigate.

Liz: And work didn't end at dark. You could have an eight-hour day.

Sandy: Solar system interests me more, but I don't really know that I'd want to make up the kit.

Heidi: It is hard to make it hands on too.

Marilyn: I'll tell you, if you do the solar system, you'll hear me pushing a lot for a moon journal, for measuring time by the sun.

Liz: Which we did some stuff from …

Rich: Yeah, operation physics.

Sandy: I bought those things when we went through that.

Liz: Oh, did you?

Marilyn: That's how you do hands on things with that kind of thing, in my opinion.

Liz: There's a guy in Decatur who does a lot of science work-shops and does a lot with space. I can't remember his name, but he gave me some stuff. Like with a lamp and a styrofoam ball and how you turn off all the other lights and get your room dark and how you can see the phases of the moon on that styrofoam ball and I going wow you can. That's cool.

Marilyn:	And then you've got to watch it at night and really see it before it really means anything. You know someone asked me a few years ago. We saw the moon one night and we were talking about it and they said well where do you think its going to be this time of day a week from now? Do you know? I don't either, I mean I didn't then I didn't even know how to figure it out, so I had to watch. What did it look like.
Liz:	And he had us frost cookies to learn the phases of the moon.
Jake:	Ok, that does it for me. (We all laugh.)
Heidi:	Can we just leave that blank and say we're working on that this year?
Marilyn:	We've got a year, but we'll work on it this year.
Rich:	Well, can we see a book for land and water. Ok, Sandy, I wasn't going to say anything …
Sandy:	I didn't know we were handing this in.
Rich:	It's going to be graded.
Sandy:	What I like doing with solar system is the perspective. Measuring how far out the different solar bodies …
Liz:	He had us do that with toilet paper. Kids would love it! (She says with obvious enthusiasm in her voice.)
Sandy:	I do it by sheets of paper. Every sheet is two million, or something.
Rich:	Yeah, I did one of those. That was really interesting how we brought that down.
Liz:	It was kind of cool though with the toilet paper because everybody got their own little roll and you could see where they marked it out and Pluto was down the hall.
Rich:	What's really interesting is how you see the inner planets and it takes off after that.
Marilyn:	What's really interesting is when you do that with geologic time, where humans fit in.
Rich:	I wonder if that is a little over fourth grader's heads.
Heidi:	That was the problem that I think third grade found and decided not to do this unit.
Marilyn:	That's why solar systems is such a hard thing to do. So much of it that is very abstract.
Heidi:	One thing about it, the kids are so interested in it.
Rich:	They are interested in it, like dinosaurs.
Liz:	Oh, they are interested in it.
Marilyn:	And if we decide to do it, and I don't think it's a reason not to do it. But, if we do it we have to really, really have

> to keep this on a concrete level as we possibly can even though it is theoretical ideas we have to keep it somehow or another keep it concrete. (Others agree.)
>
> **Heidi:** So for the fourth unit we can just put "to be developed this year"?
>
> **Marilyn:** Or we can put solar system question mark.
>
> **Liz:** Or land and water question mark or land and water slash solar system.
>
> **Sandy:** Maybe we need to look at the land and water books again.
>
> **Rich:** Definitely.

In this conversation ideas that teachers had about choosing a topic were clarified by each other and by Marilyn as she directed the conversation. This idea of choosing a topic is more than just picking the content to teach. Some of the aspects of making decisions about what to teach included things like teacher interest ("I am more interested in solar system" or "that topic interested us the least."), student interest ("Kids really like space."), their previous teaching experiences and also learning experiences with the topics and activities, what kinds of ideas the kids in their grade would probably be capable of learning (concrete vs. abstract concepts), and how the ideas of the unit fit into the standards (Were the topics covering a wide span of scientific areas—physical, earth, and life sciences?). The fourth grade did decide to do solar systems after several of the teachers put together activities and ideas that they collected and tried them out during the next school year.

The conversation about choosing a topic of study exemplifies aspects of the idea of community conversation or "collaborative conversation" that Hollingsworth described (see Chapter 2). These fourth grade teachers came to the planning meeting, not only to make decisions about what steps needed to be taken next for their own fourth grade curriculum, but also to continue the conversation that they had been having since the outset of the changing science curriculum. This conversation moved between deciding what to teach, how to teach, how the activities went, where this teaching and learning fit in to their previous teaching and learning experiences and continued between formal scheduled meetings. Teachers discussed these things, as teachers do, in the context of their daily teaching experiences with each other, with their principals, and with me as I visited their classrooms. Within the context of their own personal teaching experiences teachers were able to clarify the ideas about the curricular and pedagogical changes in the context of their classrooms and in their own space.

Support for Doing Science and Teaching Science: Positive Learning to Positive Teaching?

During the second summer science camp, we again met at Marilyn's home for the teacher portion of the course. In the first week we set up a study of the environments surrounding Marilyn's home. She lives in a beautiful environment which includes a pond, a river bottom, natural prairie, and wooded areas. These would be the settings for our learning and the inquiries that we proposed. The major assignment for the teachers was to complete a nature study. The purpose for this inquiry was for the teachers to become an expert on a topic after studying it closely for a week. We hoped that they would become challenged with seeing something new, unique, and compelling in the topic that they chose and that they would become active learners and questioning scientists, researchers, artists, and writers. We wanted them to see how art, language arts, and science could be integrated and we especially wanted to model an inquiry learning project. Each teacher chose a topic and completed five art and five writing activities, a list of questions that they encountered while engaging in their inquiry (and brief answers to at least three of the questions), and a reflection paper about their learning experience, what and how they learned and thoughts about the process of keeping a journal of this type.

The teachers chose a variety of topics for their studies: a tree in their front yard, a bird nest built on their porch lamp, the cows in their pasture, the moon, cattails in Marilyn's pond, hummingbirds feeding from a feeder, crickets kept in a terrarium, the moon, bees in a flower garden, pepper plants in a vegetable garden. They chose their topics because of interest, convenience, or because it was something they wanted to try with their classes in the following school year. When we shared the journals at their completion, many of the teachers expressed disappointment that the study did not last longer than a week. Not one teacher complained about the experience and almost every one of them expressed positive feeling about looking at an aspect of nature closely—a topic of their choice—and their own surprise at how attached they felt to their inquiry. One teacher wrote in her journal:

> When I first began this journal, I felt totally lost. I had never participated in a project of this type, and did not fell capable of doing so. I was amazed at the prospect of doing this with children. I guess overwhelmed is the most appropriate description.
>
> Each night after coming inside from watching the squirrel, I would jot down questions I had, and look through the books I had for answers. I found myself coming up with more questions even as I found some of the answers. My involvement in the project seemed to be deepening without

intent. I began looking out the window every time I went into my kitchen to see if the squirrel was back yet. I read up on what the squirrel's habits were, when they mate, their offspring, what varieties there are, how they live, where they live, and even how long they survive. The more I learned, the more I felt I knew about this friend, and the more comfortable I felt with the project.

I grew up in a suburb of Chicago, and quiet honestly, have always taken the nature around me for granted. This was the first time that I had actually studied any part of it and realized the role of the animals and the plants in the whole picture.

Another teacher wrote about her experience observing happenings in her garden:

I enjoyed taking time to just watch the bees at work in my flowerbed. This was an experience I had not given myself prior to this assignment. While taking time to observe the bees, I also enjoyed other sights and sounds. I had not noticed the variety of birds that live close to our house. The sounds they were making were soothing to my ear. We have many rabbits, but I had not noticed them in this new more natural way. I spend many hours working in my flower garden and taking care of the landscaping around our home, but I now have a new appreciation for their beauty and the necessities these plants provide for many small creatures.

My senses seemed to come alive, and I made clear, less inhibited notation. Questions about what I was seeing came very easily. I thought to myself, this must be what very young children experience on a daily basis. I found this experience to be powerful and very enjoyable. I plan to continue using this investigative process in my classroom as well as at home with my six-year-old son.

I explain in detail the project and the feelings that the teachers had about this inquiry project because these nature journals became an example of the ways that individual spaces for learning can translate into classroom changes. The teachers wrote positively and enthusiastically about their own experiences with the nature journal. Many of the teachers, perhaps because of their own positive learning experiences, tried out some of the inquiry ideas, writing ideas, art ideas, or in general journal ideas in the summer science camp that they taught.

They [the students] successfully used the journals. It was not as difficult for them as I thought it might be. I especially like the journal work where they have to predict and then record the results. They continue to be enthused about the powders.

The same teacher wrote about another day, continuing to focus on the use of journals in her summer science camp classroom.

> Today they [the students] were a little "looser" but still were focused. One thing that I am pleasantly surprised about is the use of their journals. Again today they drew a chart, wrote predictions and then results. They do not object to doing this and then they refer back to it in our discussion.

This teacher was surprised about the interest that the children had in keeping a journal of their observations and then using the journal to share their thoughts and results. The same teacher wrote in her own journal:

> I really enjoyed doing something for the sake of doing it, for example the centers on the parts of the plants at Marilyn's and the nature journals. I liked being challenged to look at things that are all around me in a new way. I'd like to provide these kinds of times for my students. I need time to be able to ask questions until I understand. I sometimes forget that in the classroom.

Again, I do not give these examples as a testimony to our in-service teaching skills. Although the teachers generally had a very positive experience with the nature journal project and many of these teachers did try aspects of the project in their own teaching, I can only say that there seems to be a relationship between the two events. Even if a teacher has a positive experience with a science activity or a type of learning tool such as the nature journal, it does not necessarily mean that this experience will transfer into positive teaching experiences or even that the teacher will try the pedagogy with their own students. Teachers trying out science themselves (and having a positive experience with that science) does give them a new perspective on the learning and teaching. Their own learning experience provides one more aspect of the learning and teaching that they can consider when making choices and decisions about what and how science will be taught in their own classrooms.

In their final reflection papers for the course teachers were asked to tell what kinds of goals that they had for their own science teaching in the upcoming school year. Again many of the teachers referred to their own journal experience and how they would like to create that kind of integration, excitement, interest, and connection to learning for the students in their classes.

> I use journaling frequently in my classroom, but not invitations [the writing and art activities that encourage observation and inquiry]. I like how these lend a change of pace to the daily "reporting."

> The cinquain and concrete poems were very successful with the chemical unit. I will do that next year. I would like to have students try a rebus story in the rocks unit and a story from a naturalist's viewpoint for the plant unit. I

would also like to expand on the drawings we did in our simple machines unit. I want to give them more time to do journal entries.

As I look ahead to the school year and teaching the science kits, I want to spend more time on the journals. Last year students had notebooks for each unit of study that handouts and worksheets were kept in. At the end of the unit they were bound together so the kids had a book to take home. I didn't spend a lot of time on writing. Next year I want to include more writing of observations, reflections, poetry, and make it an integral part of the unit. I would like it to be more like our nature journals that we did instead of a notebook full of pages copied from a manual.

Spaces, safe spaces, where tests scores do not matter and where parents, colleagues, and administrators knew that trying out science ideas was the goal of the teaching and learning, were created as part of the summer science camp. In fact, creating a space for trying out ideas was the purpose for this teacher course. By trying out a model of inquiry teaching, the teachers were able to experience, question, and reflect on how their students might learn in a similar manner. The space of teaching in the summer science camp classroom gave teachers an opportunity to act out their teaching ideas and try them out in a safe space. "I really felt that the students learned without added pressure which is not always the case during the school year. The students in our class did the experiments just to find out something, not to find a certain answer, or know the information for a test." I think the teachers learned about themselves and the science teaching in much the same way. The journaling also became a space for teachers to sort out their thoughts and ideas in a relatively private manner. During this project we tried to provide these concrete spaces, but set them up in such a way that the ultimate space was an individual space for teachers to think about their learning and teaching experiences and come to conclusions about their effectiveness for themselves. This is a conceptual space that teachers use to make decisions about how teaching reforms will be enacted in the space of their own classroom.

A teacher's classroom is her own, but the space is created by a mosaic of influences. Teachers do not work in their own creative vacuum, but they do have influence over the patterns that emerge and which themes are present in the foreground of their work. These stories show that teachers can and do make decisions about the creative process of teaching, work to make changes in their practice, and do make decisions about the ways that these processes are enacted within their classrooms. The ways that they implement the change process is a personal one and because it is a personal process, school reform efforts largely depend on the teachers making these efforts a part of their own thinking, teaching, and learning. By giving teachers a space to understand their conceptions about science

learning, teachers learn to articulate their own philosophy of education—
what they think about the curricular and pedagogical reforms. As the
teachers tried "doing" the science themselves, reflecting on this experience, and then trying the processes with children they begin to form their
own understanding of the curricular and pedagogical changes.

Paula wrote in her journal about her own teaching needs:

> Science has not been one of my favorite subjects to teach but I am finding
> that two hours of science day is a bit much for me. I am enjoying the topics
> but the amount of preparation for the activities and the format of working
> in groups the majority of the time is wearing on me. I need more of a bal-
> ance of activities and some independent work time.

It is interesting to note that in the discussions that we had after class each
day, Paula highlighted some of the activities that they had done in their
second grade room—the kinds of activities that she mentioned in these
conversations and also throughout her journal incorporated science with
language arts—which is an area that she wanted to focus on (unlike science, which she says she does not enjoy teaching). Again from her journal, "Next year I want to include more writing of observations, reflections,
poetry, and make it an integral part of the science unit." Paula created a
way to make the science teaching something that she can be more interested in working through. She will combine it with a subject that she
enjoys as well as structure the learning so that her need as a teacher are
also met. She has created an understanding of the new pedagogy and curriculum that is her own.

SUPPORTING TEACHERS:
A PERSONAL PROCESS AMIDST GROUP CHANGE

When this school district made the public commitment to make change in
its pedagogical processes and its curriculum, Balmoral schools also made
a commitment in time, finances, and effort in promoting change and
ongoing in-service for its teachers. This effort was begun informally
before I became involved, and as the project unfolded there was a great
deal of support from the district administration in providing resources.
Teachers were given release time to attend planning meetings and in-service, the district did hire a part-time science clerk to facilitate the organizing and managing of supplies and materials, space was allocated for
storage of those supplies and materials as well as for the summer science
camp. These kinds of support are very tangible and concrete and easy to
implement, but these supports are not enough to facilitate real and lasting change. I believe that without teachers making a commitment to the

changes, the curricular and pedagogical reform efforts will not have real and lasting impact on the teaching and learning. The teachers in their own classrooms have the power to make reform efforts succeed or fail. Teachers are the "foundation for any long-term solutions" (Fullan & Hargreaves, 1996, p. 64). For this reason, they need to feel a genuine part of the reform efforts, and understand for themselves the whys and the hows of changing. Why is this a better method of teaching? How will this information be better understood by the kids in my classroom? Why should I do something different when the scores of my tests are high right now? The stories in this chapter show the ways that the supports constructed externally helped the teachers internally conceptualize changing their practices in ways that they could be comfortable teaching and ideas that they are willing to incorporate into their classroom practice.

By assembling and surrounding themselves with the ideas, the experiences, and the materials that they are comfortable with, teachers create a space that they are comfortable teaching and learning in. Nesting is a concept traditionally thought of as a practice by women. It is "the sporadic assemblage of small bits and pieces, woven together, arranged correctly, until you are comfortable sitting amidst them ... in the mistaken belief that this will make everyone happy and safe" (Quindlen, 1988, p. 43). If you imagine making a home, a place where you have gathered the things that make you comfortable—the people you are comfortable around, books and items that you enjoy, food that you have prepared—all of which can challenge you in various ways, but which you surround yourself with to provide a sense of safety. "The altogether trivial assemblage of those small parts that make up life for many of us. Nesting has been traditionally undervalued. This is because nesting has largely been the purview of women" (p. 41). It may seem simple to structure school reform so that teachers can assemble the materials that they need, the resources that they need, and the support that they need—these are some of the ways that teachers can feel "safe" in a time of change, where their ideas of what teaching and learning are challenged. By providing structures like time for conversation and reflection and by carving out spaces for teachers to try out ideas, teachers can formulate ideas of reform that they are comfortable accepting, adapting, and using in their own classrooms.

By providing time and space—both concretely and conceptually—to figure out their own answers to these questions, we give teachers a reason to want to change or to not want to change. It is ultimately a personal process which certainly can be enhanced and facilitated by supporting that process with structural supports. But those supports must allow for the individuals to work through their doubts, their excitement, their own ideas. The supports need to celebrate and embrace the power of the individual teacher in reform efforts.

NOTE

1. Each of the science units that the teachers taught was assembled as a kit (or tub). In the tub were all of the needed supplies, materials, tools, equipment, and so forth, to teach their class the unit on the designated science topic. Some of the units were bought prepacked from a company and others were assembled by the teachers and, in the second year of the project, by the district science clerk.

CHAPTER 5

COLLABORATION AND OWNERSHIP

WHAT IS COLLABORATION?: PRODUCT AND PROCESS

Because collaborations play a role in the ways that ownership of a project is enacted, I will spend some time discussing what it means to collaborate—what it means to work together in partnerships for reform. In the following sections, I will describe and discuss ideas of collaboration between researchers and teachers.

We hear the word collaboration in many different contexts. It is a word that teachers, administrators, and educational researchers use to mean "working with others." But, people work together in many different ways. There are issues of leadership, power, and agenda to consider. Who sets the terms of the collaboration? For what means and to what ends is the collaboration set up? When and how will the collaboration exist? My own understanding of the term as it relates to teacher research and curriculum reform combines parts of two theoretical frameworks—feminist and traditional.

A Feminist View of Collaborative Relationships

Collaborative relationships are one of the defining characteristics of doing feminist research. The ways that the research is conducted with the participants (process) is as important, if not more important, than the

---

Teachers and the Reform of Elementary Science, 89–106
Copyright © 2004 by Information Age Publishing
All rights of reproduction in any form reserved.

outcomes of the research project (product). The process itself is the way that power is negotiated, change is made, and reflective learning occurs. Lather (1991) uses her methodology to design research that includes three interwoven issues: (1) the need for reciprocity, (2) theory-building instead of theory imposition, and (3) the question of validity. It is part of her mission to create projects that bring "empowering approaches to research where both the researcher and the researched become the changer and the changed" (p. 56). The researcher does not come to the project with neutrality, but comes ready to collaborate. The researcher brings a "praxis-oriented" model that acts on the desire for people to gain self-understanding and self-determination both in the research and in their daily lives. The research should guide the researched in coming to a change through self-reflexivity and learning to understand their own situation. The researcher is not a speaker for the researched, but someone who can help take away the barriers that prevent them from speaking for themselves. Collaborative relationships between the researched and the researcher provide the agent for change as they mutually understand and define problems and solutions. In praxis-oriented inquiry, reciprocally educative process is more important than product as empowering methods contribute to consciousness-raising and transformative social action. Through dialogue and reflexivity, design, data, and theory emerge, with data being recognized as generated from people in a relationship. The design emerges from the people in a relationship (Lather, 1991).

Hollingsworth (1994) utilizes a feminist framework in her research, but much like myself, did not decide beforehand that was her aim. She writes that is just felt "correct." She began the research journey not knowing what to name the method, but it seemed to fit in the feminist traditions. She found that collaborative conversations gave voice to underpowered individuals (teachers); it involves inquiry based in women's needs, and; there was an equal vulnerability between the researcher and the researched—there did not exist the voice of authority, but was also open to critical examination.

Collaboration as Support: Lisa's Story

Lisa teaches first grade and has been teaching for over 10 years. She had been working with the science curriculum changes since the inception of the project. Lisa sent me the following e-mail in September 1999.

HELP!!! I need help with my science lessons. Today's lesson of sorting by shape and color did not go well- what a surprise! I just assumed this group could do something simple like that—especially after the GREAT discussion we had on Wed. about solids. I'm going to try the next lessons on stacking and rolling next week. Would you be available to help next Wed. 12:15-1:30 and Friday 2-3?

Lisa

I met Lisa in the hall as her kids were coming out of the bathroom. I followed the class to their room. As the kids were getting situated in their desks, Lisa introduced me to two other adults who met us at the door. One was her student teacher and one was the first grade aide.[1] I was surprised to see the other adults as Lisa's e-mail had seemed in a panic, as if things were totally out of control and she needed help with the kids. She seemed to want an extra set of hands. After the lesson, though, I saw that she wanted something else from me—support for her efforts and reassurance that the teaching and learning were going well. As soon as the kids were out of the room she asked me, " How do you think it went?"

I really wanted to honor Lisa's request to come to her science class. I had been talking to Lisa briefly in the halls and after school when I had visited other teachers in the building for the past year. I had also worked with her during summer science camp and felt that we had a fairly candid and friendly relationship. In her journal she had been honest with me and her writings had led to some discussion between us about the ordering of supplies and the way teachers work together. She had filled me in on personalities of teachers and had seemed genuinely motivated and interested in trying the new science curriculum. She was enthusiastic and encouraging to her teammates in the first grade. I also think that Lisa felt confident in her teaching and in the way that things were going with the science lessons and units. When a teacher is teaching in her classroom by herself, the only things that she can share about her teaching are stories. Teachers, when talking to other teachers, can only talk about what happened, they have not shared the teaching experience in most cases. When I visited classrooms as another set of hands, another adult who was a part of the science reform efforts, it could be perceived as sharing the experience. The teachers were eager to talk about the way things went with someone who was there and could understand what they were talking about, someone who had all the reference points that they described, someone who could share the frustrations and the highs of the particular lesson.

Lisa's use of our collaborative relationship, I think, shows some aspects of what Hollingsworth describes. As the researcher, I was not in her classroom to show her the "right" way to teach, but I was there to support her in her efforts to make changes in her teaching and in a manner that she was comfortable with. We used conversation to explore her feelings, to examine the classroom experiences, and to push changes forward. By sharing a classroom experience our conversation had shared reference points.

A Traditional View of Collaboration

A traditional sense of collaboration (as I am naming it here) has many of the same aspects of working together as the feminist points of view discussed: creating space for dialogue, working to bring every participant's view to the table and level the playing field, and trying to bring about change. Although these aspects are present, they may not be the hallmark characteristics of the research. The framing of the research projects are different, roles are named, and specific plans of action are in place. The change, or the outcome of the research project, is the main concern. The focus of the research is not on the process of the project, not on the power of the teachers, not on looking at the women's standpoint, and not on creating social change through a shift in power. These may be outgrowths of the action taken by the teams of teachers and researchers as collaborative conversations are held, as teachers become part of the decision-making process, and as the role of teacher and research shift and change. When Clift, Veal, Holland, Johnson, McCarthy (1995) began their project, the roles of the participating groups were clearly defined as three groups of individuals coming together to promote school reform—university researchers, school administrators, and teachers.

> [But, they] were forced to think of research activity in a new way. We could not assume the role of educational expert, and we were not willing to create divisions between those who create knowledge and those who use knowledge. Therefore, ... the school participants had a role in naming, framing, and solving the educational problems under investigation.... [N]ew relationships and roles would need to develop. (p. 6)

The science reform effort that we were a part of in Balmoral holds several aspects of this traditional framework. We came into the project with specific roles—the university staff members, the administrators, and the teachers. Our roles evolved as we reassessed the project and its goals and worked together to help the teachers implement the curriculum. Although many of the teachers believed in the outcome and processes of an inquiry-based science program, and some were the impetus for the change, many teachers felt that their voices and their ideas were not a part of this curricular change. They were happy with the status quo. As these teachers tried out some of the activity-based units, they voiced their opinions and new objectives and goals were put in place to meet some of their needs. Clandinin and Connelly (1992) address the importance of giving teachers a space to share the stories of their experience and how it relates to the researcher.

A sense of equity between participants is particularly important in narrative inquiry. However, in researcher-practitioner relationships where practitioners have long been silenced through being used as objects for study.... Practitioners have experienced themselves as without voice in the research process and may find it difficult to feel empowered to tell their stories. They have been made to feel less than equal. (p. 4)

Researchers working with teachers need to create spaces and forums for the teachers to have a voice in the process of change. The researcher needs to be concerned with the process of change, and how that change may or may not occur, rather than only concerned that change occurs. The product of change is the "common goal" and the individual stories may not be heard.

How Do I Interpret these Frameworks in My Own Understanding of Collaboration and Collaborative Research?

Although changing the science curriculum from a text-oriented approach to a more inquiry and hands-on learning approach was the common goal of the reform efforts described in this project, the process of that change was what I tried to concentrate on. Change is not something that could be located to a specific event in this project, but something that occurred (and is on-going) throughout the project and in varying degrees and depths. Change is a process.

By looking at the way that I see my own self as a researcher and the way that I construct relationships with those that I am working with on a research project (teachers in the classroom), I see the relationships very much like the relationships that I have with my close long-term female friends. We know about one another, we have a sense of trust, there is a comfortableness to talk about our successes and failures—to share the smallest of details of our lives and also to celebrate the big moments. We can sit over a cup of coffee and talk about the things in our experience that are serious to us—that have meaning for us. At times some of these topics may not be important, but they give us insight to each other and build a context for knowing one another. Sometimes we take and sometimes we give. Sometimes we come to a friendship with a goal in mind and sometimes we are there for the companionship. Sometimes we are the experts, other times we are the novice learners. In all cases we travel the journey of the relationship together, trying to understand our experiences and each other as we go.

Clift et al. (1995) use a metaphor of a dinner party in describing their perspective on collaboration. In this metaphor the researcher is a dinner guest in the home of the school and those who live there (teachers, administrators, etc.).

> The researchers often seek adoption as occasional and transitory members of the family. They agree to help with the dishes, cook a few meals, and tidy up when asked to do so. They also open themselves to the family as their private worlds become somewhat intertwined with family events.... They cannot claim to be objective and unaffected by the occupants of the house, for as these researchers become more intimately connected with practice, practice informs and shapes both the research and the researchers. (p. 4)

If I extend the metaphor to describe the feminist standpoint on collaborative research relationships, it would look something like this: The researchers and the teachers meet. They decide that they are hungry and would like to eat so the teachers invite the researchers to their home. On the way they decide what they are going to prepare and they stop by the grocery store to collect the ingredients. Everyone helps in the preparation, the researchers know which cupboards hold the spices and where the oven mitts are kept. It is difficult to tell who's home it is because everyone seems equally comfortable. The dinner is made and the guests and homeowners enjoy the food and conversation. Everyone cleans up.

My own dinner guest metaphor would fall somewhere in the middle of the two. I feel that it is important for all parties to have a say in the outcome of the project, that each member should have a voice, and that the process should be empowering. I also believe that some realities of school and university research partnerships limit the ways that research can be enacted in the public schools. We have to be careful that we do not impose our needs as researchers before those of teachers.

COLLABORATIVE SPACES: LINGERING QUESTIONS

The story told here has been my story. It has been the story of the way that I frame my understanding of collaboration and its place in teacher research and where I fit in as a researcher in the process of narrative inquiry. The use of narrative in teacher research leaves me with some questions. What happens when I move from my own narrative and work to craft the story of the teachers with which I have worked? Can these two narratives be separated? Should they be separate stories? Whose narrative do I write? Does the narrative empower teachers?

> Narrative explanation, in practice, means that one person's voice—the writer's—speaks for that of others ... narrators often speak about and for constituencies to which they do not belong. These practices, of course, raise

postmodernist issues about the researcher's authority and privilege. For whom do we speak, with what voice, to what end, using what criteria?... Wherever text is being produced there is the question of what social, power, and sexual relationships of production are being reproduced. How does our writing reproduce a system of domination, and how does it challenge that system? What right do we have to speak for others? To write their lives? (Richardson, 1990, pp. 26-27)

Richardson suggests that we recognize the researcher as a narrator who has one perspective of the narrative to share. The researcher is "a person with a point of view; an embodied person responsible for his or her words ... another point of view" (pp. 26-27).

Grumet (1990) also speaks to this question. She asks, "So where does that leave us, educational researchers who read other people's stories in order to improve communities we do not really share with them?" (p. 321) Teachers have taken risks in telling their knowledge to us. They cannot know how we will understand them, how the stories will be perceived, or if they will be listened to.

I suspect that the difference between personal and impersonal knowledge, or practical and impractical knowledge is not a difference in what it is we know, but how we tell it and to whom. Personal knowledge in this scheme is constituted by the stories about experience we usually keep to ourselves, and practical knowledge, by the stories that are never, or rarely related, but provide, nevertheless the structure for the improvisations that we call coping, problem-solving action. (p. 322)

Because the stories have been told, "it marks the territory that is to be the ground for meaningful action.... Its action is perceptible because it is framed by a beginning, middle, and end" (pp. 320-321).

I am not sure that I agree with Grumet when she talks about those of us who work with the narratives of teachers. She states that "we too have been teachers, and our fascination with the life of school where we no longer teach, with the challenges and burdens that we no longer bear, is suspect. Whose stories are we studying? Whose experience are we interpreting?" (p. 323) I do agree with the way that she views her work and I like the phrase she uses to examine her interpretations, "Look what they've done to my song, Mom" (p. 323). Grumet says, "If my work permits the teachers I work with to examine their own work with a seeing that is more inclusive, that surveys an ever widening surround, that is a search I would gladly join" (p. 324). I want the stories that I write to be narratives that are an honest and accurate telling of the experiences of teachers— tellings that the teachers trust me to tell. I am not ready to say that my research is suspect as Grumet says.

Bateson also discusses the importance of establishing collaborative relationships and the ways that researchers view the researched:

> The words used by social scientists for those they involve in their research feel wrong to me, even though ... I believe that the people we call "informants" are our truest colleagues. These women are not "interviewees," not "subjects" in an experiment, not "respondents" to a questionnaire. There is symmetry in our mutual recognition but there is asymmetry in that I am the one who goes off and weaves our separate skeins of memory into a single fabric. But they weave me into their different projects, too. (Bateson, 1989, p. 101)

Hopefully, the impact of my research has been positive and woven into the experience of the teachers' work as their experiences are woven into my work. It is sure that our interactions have impacted each other; collaborations play a role in the ways that ownership of a project is enacted. The questions that remain for me are not easy ones to answer. Researchers involved in collaborative projects have an interesting balance to find. Many efforts of educational reform are funded by outside sources and many "outsiders" have worthy contributions to make to reform efforts. I believe that we must find ways to acknowledge "the ways of knowing" teachers have and celebrate the ways that they integrate their experiences, their understandings and their actions as teaching and learning in their classrooms. Teachers will find ways to create ownership of reform projects and make the reform efforts work for them and for their students. In the following sections, I will explore ways that I saw teachers take ownership of a science curriculum many perceived as imposed.

IMPOSING A CURRICULUM

It is spring 2000, and the science project will end after the summer science camp. The science committee meets for one of the last times. We meet as we have met all during this year in the district's conference room after school for about an hour. It is actually an empty classroom that sits across from the superintendent's office that not only serves as a meeting room, but also a district storage room. Seven teachers representing various grade levels and the three buildings involved in the science curriculum changes, the district curriculum coordinator, Marilyn and myself are present. We sit around three large tables situated in a T-shape.

Marilyn leads the discussion. Today the agenda is to talk about the topic decisions that each grade level has made, start discussions of the summer science camp, discuss any concerns or topics that the teacher representations want to bring up, and list recommendations for continuation of the program. There is a firm commitment by the school board, the administration, and the teachers to continue the science program. The consensus, despite the concerns voiced by the teachers and discussed in previous chapters, is that the move from a text-oriented approach to the hands-on inquiry approach has generally been a positive one for the district and that the teachers want to continue working in this direction with their students.

Some representative comments about the changes by teachers:

> "I like this. I am a bit concerned however that students aren't getting a more 'rounded' science education. Perhaps if we could condense the units and work with other areas of science as well."

> "I am satisfied with this program. I would not want to return to the textbook. I am concerned that we are limited to 3 or 4 topics. The yearly achievement tests will assume the students have experiences with many more areas."

> "The students and I both like this way of teaching."

> "I think that there should be a balance between using the texts and the kits. This would enhance our science program to incorporate both styles. This would also ensure that we are teaching to different learning types."

> "I would not want to return to the textbook! I am very satisfied with this program."

> "I'm encouraged by the results so far of this new science program, but I'm interested in how our test scores will come out. I know we shouldn't teach to the test, but our effectiveness will be judged in this manner."

In preparation for meeting and in acting on a statement that she had made over and over in working with the teachers and administrators, Marilyn had prepared a report of "recommendations for sustained program growth and support." She had said repeatedly while working with the teachers and administrators that the changes needed to be believed in and supported by both the teachers and by the administration if any sustained change was to occur. In other words, the district needed to take ownership. In a matter of a few months, the district would need to be ready to fully take charge of the ideas, growth, and support of the program—both conceptually and concretely. During this meeting we went through some of the main points Marilyn had documented in her report.

She wanted to give these recommendations to the superintendent and the school board, and wanted to get the committee's feedback and ideas before doing so. Her report and the ideas that we discussed in that meeting reflected many of the concerns that teachers had voiced in working with the new program. She told the teachers that these were ideas for consideration only, that they were by no means the only way to continue the program, but from her understanding of their school district and how things worked there, she thought these would be effective structures.

Some of the main points included the following: (1) The need for a science program coordinator who would basically take over the role that Marilyn had taken. This person would take care of the logistics of the program including chairing the district science committee, organizing meetings for teachers to continue exchanges of ideas about the science curriculum, and also oversee the record keeping of the program (materials, finances, etc). (2) A continuation of the district science committee would serve as a basis for conversation and communication between grade levels and between elementary school buildings. The members of this committee would also represent the grade level teachers or their building in making complaints and suggestions, as well as ideas and concerns to the administration, the science clerk, and other teachers on the committee. (3) Classroom teachers' continued involvement in the discussion about the science program—relating problems, attending meetings, communicating about supplies and materials, curriculum and pedagogy. (4) The need to keep a science clerk who keeps track of supplying and maintaining the science tubs.

These four items were outlined for the administration and there was a consensus of the committee members that by writing these down on paper for the district administration, a sense of priority and a sense of stability for the program would continue. In other words, by writing it down, it would become more real and it would be more likely that follow-though would occur.

The teachers also came to an agreement that they would like each grade level to create a few science mini-units for their use. These mini-units would be short, one to two week units on topics that the teachers felt were left out of the new curriculum—topics that they felt the kids need to have a background in mainly because the topics appeared on the achievement tests and also because they felt that the topics were part of a well-rounded curriculum. But, the teachers did not want to leave the choice of topics completely up to each classroom teacher's discretion. A member of the committee expressed these feelings,

> One of the reasons we wanted to work on our science curriculum in the first place was because there wasn't any communication and people weren' t fol-

lowing what was in their books. Some teachers would skip topics and some teachers would elaborate and do things that were already done in other grades so the kids just ended up with hit and miss depending on the teacher they had. We need to make sure that we don't end up doing that again, where teachers just add what they want and we end up with hit and miss and repetition.

The idea of mini-units became one that teachers were very happy with and one that they continued to discuss. They liked the way that it presented what they considered to be a balance of teaching methods. It gave them an opportunity to keep enjoying what they liked about the hands on learning, but also gave them an opportunity to control some of the knowledge (by teaching out of the book, or teaching concepts directly, or teaching the topics they felt were left out of the new curriculum) gained by their students. They could return (or keep with) methods that they were comfortable with and therefore could teach topics that they knew their students had learned about in the past and in the past had done well on the tests. These mini-units would be in their own control and would give them a sense of safety.

After the meeting ended, I walked to the parking lot with two of the teachers. I asked them what their feelings were about the recommendations and what the future would hold for the science program.

David: This is the first time that I felt like our ideas were really represented. I know that we've been talking about a lot of this stuff for a while, but I didn't think that anyone was really listening.

Jake: Yeah, I really like the ideas of the mini-units. I think that will help.

David: That makes me feel better about the whole thing and that we are going to work out the topics between grade levels.

Jake: That will give us a better coverage of science.

David: I feel like we are really working towards a good program now.

Maybe it was the fact that we (Marilyn and I) would not be a part of the program anymore and that the teachers could see that end coming, but after that particular meeting it seemed that they felt more in control of the program, that the program would go in the direction that they had chosen. They were very interested and satisfied with the idea of adding mini-units to the science curriculum. They felt that this would allow them to cover some of the content that might appear on the tests and that they felt they were leaving out presently. The teachers also liked the idea that they would continue to meet as a committee and that this committee would continue to set up meetings for on-going conversation about the curriculum—concerns, needs, supplies, and just general communication between grade levels to keep the scope and sequence of the science curriculum intact. The committee would also have to decide how or if to continue the summer science camp which had become very a very popular public relations tool for the administration because of the community's support of the program. These concerns were of importance to the teachers and they could see that they would have the lead voice in seeing how they would be carried out in the future of their own science program, one that would be contained in their own district now.

The teachers had put much effort and time into the changes. There had been much time imposed on them to think about the program and to talk about the program. Even though this time was carved out for them to make decisions about how they wanted to proceed with the curriculum and to make decisions about the resources and supplies that they needed—the space was carved out *for* them, not *by* them. This makes a difference in how most of the teachers viewed the reform efforts—it was presented to them, not instigated by them.

Although there were many opportunities for teachers to voice their concerns and ideas throughout the implementation of the new science curriculum, this curriculum had been imposed on the majority of the teachers. The district science committee made many of the initial decisions and then these choices were presented to the other teachers in their grade level and in their buildings. How can teachers "own" a project, make it their own, and believe in the ideas of the reform when the initial efforts were not their own? They did not choose to make the changes or necessarily feel that changes even needed to be made. And in some cases, they felt that changes needed to be made but perhaps not the changes that were set into motion by the science committee. These dilemmas were present throughout the project and manifested themselves in individual teachers' classroom practice. Paris (1993, p. 10) describes the problem of teacher participation in curricular decisions under this model:

> [F]rom the perspective of the classroom teacher, teacher representation on curriculum committees does not necessarily professionalize or alter individual teachers' relationships to curriculum. The individual classroom teacher who did not serve on the committee, or the committee representative who held a minority opinion, is still expected to implement curricula created or selected by someone other than herself. She has neither been empowered or professionalized.

In the following stories I will try to show that some teachers did feel a disconnect to the new program; it was not theirs. Other teachers found an easy connection to the changes. I will show ways that I did or did not see ownership of the reforms taking place in classrooms and share conversations that also exemplify the ways that teachers made or did not make the project "theirs."

Part of the dilemma of a project like this that involves outside individuals like a consultant and like a university researcher is that these individuals are seen as outsiders coming in to "fix" the problems, introduce new ideas, and then make sure that the curriculum and pedagogy are implemented in the classroom. In this particular case, I don't think that either Marilyn, Margery or myself presented ourselves in that manner nor had those kinds of ideas about our own roles in the project, but that is one perception that having outside personnel be a part of the change process brings to a reform effort. The perception of the teachers is what ultimately mattered—they were the individuals who would or would not take the reform efforts and embrace them in ways that would make them work in their own classroom.

Researchers and those involved with the reforms need to be aware of the process of change and not only the product of change. Voices of the teachers need to be heard throughout reform efforts. This is what David was telling me when he said that he felt no one had heard any of the ideas and concerns he had been talking about for over a year (not enough breadth, leaving out topics). He felt that the administration and Marilyn were only concerned about the implementation of the program, in getting the teachers to teach four units of science. "I know that they are for the program and they had told me before that we couldn't teach more than four units during a year. Now they have changed their mind on that." He wanted his story to be heard as part of the process of those reform efforts.

GAIL'S STORY:
OWNERSHIP OF THE PLANNING AND TEACHING

I went into the second grade room and found the place that I usually sat in the back of the room. I helped pass out the materials when the teacher directed one of the student partners to collect something. I walked around the room helping and questioning individual pairs of students when they were working on part of the activity as the teacher gave directions. The class was working on a unit called "Changes." Today they were observing what happened to a variety of solids when they were placed in water and then when they were stirred in the water.

During the lesson, the teacher, Gail, gave very clear directions to the pairs of students working on the activities. This was a hands-on lesson but was teacher-directed. "The partner toward the window needs to get the gravel from the back table. The partner near the door can pour the gravel in the cup." These were typical instructions from Gail that continued throughout the lesson as the students created the following descriptions together. Gail wrote their ideas on the board:

1. Gravel's properties: dirty, clay, round, bumpy, cold, pink, white, blue, some brown and silver
2. Gravel's changes with water (before stirring): bubbles in water, on rocks, sank, water moves, noise, bubbles went up on top, doesn't flood
3. Gravel's changes with water (after stirring): rocks move, water is getting dirty, gravel looks purple, pond water smell, rainbow, foggy, cloudy, bubbles look like silver rings
4. Tissue's properties: smooth, white, torn, sticks together, ragged, ripped, soft, black spots, lines, holes, smashed
5. Tissue's changes in water (before stirring): floats, sinks slowly, in a ball, going apart, wet, soggy, mushy
6. Tissue's changes in water (after stirring): falling apart, mushy, soggy, foggy, cloud like, looks like ice, puffing up, feathery, fuzzy, ghosts flying in the air

Gail took all of the ideas from the students and then asked them to fill in their own description of what they observed on their own record-keeping sheets. The students completed an observational drawing as well.

After the lesson Gail and I began to talk about her experiences with the unit. One of the other second grade teachers had told her that she had done many of the extension activities and found those to be more effective and exciting learning tools. That teacher had adapted the unit herself. Gail stated that she thought it was very important to go through the unit as it was written, not having to add in other activities to elaborate and extend on ideas. She wanted to get a real feel for the curriculum and the way the authors had intended it to be taught. I asked her why she felt that way. Gail had 30 years of teaching experience. She told me that she was not an expert, that the experts had put together this unit. They had reasons for putting lessons in a certain order, for including specific lessons, for repeating concepts, and for including the information that they did. Gail was very adamant in expressing these feelings. I found this very interesting because Gail had enthusiastically accepted these changes and felt that the curriculum was engaging for both her and her students. I saw her take ownership not of the ideas in the lessons nor in the planning of the unit, but in understanding the specific lessons themselves and in the teaching of those lessons. Gail studied the teaching manual before teaching each lesson and took very detailed notes on how the lesson was supposed to take place, questions to ask, and procedures to follow. Before beginning the unit, she had completed a detailed schedule of which lessons would take two days, which lessons could be completed in one class period, and had accordingly filled in a calendar. Although Gail did allow for much student input into the discussions that followed the science activities and allowed the students to complete the activities themselves, this teacher created an ownership of the lessons by directing the procedures, the materials, and the discussions to follow her preparations.

SANDY'S STORY:
ALREADY OWNING THE IDEAS OF REFORM

For some teachers "owning" the project and the ideas of the new science curriculum was easy. These were teachers who already agreed with the hands-on pedagogy and the in-depth studying of a topic. They were teachers who already put their classes in collaborative groups for learning projects and teachers who valued ideas of integrating curriculum topics. Many of these teachers also felt very comfortable with the study of science and concepts relating to science. Sandy was an example of one of these teachers. She was a veteran teacher who had been instrumental in starting some hands-on science in her building before this project and was known as the "science expert" in her grade level, school and district meetings. She participated from the onset of the project, being one of the first teachers to pilot units as well as serving on the science committee and also in the summer science camp. The reform efforts were merely a continuation of her own science teaching ideas and interests. There were many examples of ways that she incorporated the new fourth grade topics/units into teaching ideas that she already used in her classroom. The following is an example of a lesson in which Sandy used the science information they were reading about to teach study skills.

The class had just finished observing their living things. They had created habitats for several different kinds of living things: a dwarf African frog, a fiddler crab, a snail, and guppies. The students observed the ways that the living thing had adapted to the environment in which it lived. For example, the structures of the fish that allow it to move and live in water, the structures of the crab that allow it to eat, to keep away predators, et cetera. The students had observed their animals and environment, noting any changes from their last observation in their journals, and described what they saw today. The class cleaned the tanks and fed the living things, which Sandy said she did not mind taking class time to do because of the relationship that developed between the students and their study. For the rest of the period, Sandy led the class in a shared reading of some information about the living things they were studying. The students took turns reading parts of the selection and then they were asked to decide what was the main point of the part they read. Then the class used highlighters to mark that portion of the reading.

On the surface, this continuation of the lesson sounds very traditional in its approach and that may be. What I found unique in this particular context was the way that Sandy had woven a reading/study skills lesson into the new science curriculum. She had cut and pasted parts of the background reading information provided in the teaching manual to create information packets for the students to read about their crab, fish, snails, and frogs. The kids were able to make connections between what they were observing and what they were reading. Sandy was able to reach several of her teaching goals by combining both the science and reading lessons. I had heard other teachers talk about struggling to fit all the subject and activities that needed to be taught into the time allotted for a school day. Sandy already felt comfortable with many of the pedagogies embedded in the new curriculum and was able to make connections to her own teaching goals by integrating subjects. This was a natural progression of what she already did in her classroom and made "owning" the new curriculum easier for her.

LIZ'S STORY:
TAKING OWNERSHIP BY DOING

Liz is another example of a teacher who found the new curriculum matching much of what she already believed about teaching and learning. She had no hesitation about jumping right in and trying out the new units. She saw a connection between what she was doing as a teacher and what the kids were doing in the units. "I'm learning just as much as the kids because I've never done these units before. I try to read ahead, but it doesn't make sense to me until I do it." Liz refers to reading ahead in the teaching manual and in resource books to learn about the ways that the lesson will proceed and the concepts involved, but she does not feel that she gets a good handle on the actual teaching until she has actually taught the lessons. During one of my visits to her class, the fourth graders were working on a lesson that was part of the motion and design unit. They were testing how different weights of a vehicle affected its speed. This activity involved building a vehicle and then using blocks of wood to increase or decrease the weight of the car. The kids worked in groups moving the car by adding washers to a string that was attached to the vehicle, pulling the car along a track, and timing the results with a stopwatch. What I want to emphasize is there was a lot of activity involved in the lesson and the kids really enjoyed manipulating the parts of the experiment and working with the cars. Part of the intrigue for kids in working with the hands-on science units is that they are hands-on. The kids are involved in the learning and are usually more interested in what they are doing. Liz truly believed this and was glad that the kids liked what they were doing in her class. She felt she needed to work on her teaching to get the kids to think about what they were doing. "I need to learn, too, how to work with this new curriculum. I want them to think about what they are doing. It's fun, but they need to be taught to think about what they are doing too." She was working with the students to take notes and create class charts about the results and process of their activities. By looking at the new curriculum as a learning opportunity for herself, Liz was taking ownership of the teaching and the reform efforts.

WOMEN'S WAYS OF KNOWING: TEACHERS FINDING OWNERSHIP

Belenky, Clinchy, Goldberger, and Tarule (1986) examine "women's ways of knowing." They "describe five different perspectives from which women view reality and draw conclusions about truth, knowledge and authority" (p. 3). The way that we perceive the world, participate in that world, define ourselves, interact with others, our sense of control over life events, and our views of teaching and learning are affected by our assumptions about truth, reality, and knowledge (p. 3).

> All knowledge is constructed and the knower is an intimate part of the known. At first women arrive at this insight in searching for a core of self that remains responsive to situation and context. Ultimately constructivists understand that answers to all questions vary depending on the context in which they are asked and on the frame of reference of the person doing the asking. (p. 138)

In looking at the teachers at Balmoral, and at Gail, Sandy, and Liz in particular, it is evident that they each have constructed their own way of knowing the new science curriculum and pedagogies. Gail's knowledge and understanding of teaching and learning is a blend all of her experiences as a teacher. In the instance of using the new curriculum, she relied explicitly on the "experts," those who wrote the curriculum, for the organization, the theories, and the order of the curriculum. Belenky et al. call this "received knowledge." They contend that by listening, understanding and remembering what was taught, women find power in that knowledge, thinking of themselves as someone who can learn and then pass that knowledge on to others. I believe that Gail found power in learning the new curriculum. By reading the teachers manual, organizing the activities, and following the lesson scope and sequence, Gail found that she was in control of the new curriculum and could set up the learning in her classroom in a way that she felt comfortable and in control.

Liz found that she was learning, as well, and relished in that learning. By doing—the teaching, the experimenting, the reflecting—she was able to experience the new curriculum as a teacher. The doing became her way of knowing and understanding how the curriculum would be implemented in her classroom. Belenky et al. (1986) label this knowing as subjective knowledge.

> In many ways, these women are the youths in fairy tales ... who set out from the family homestead to make their way in the world, discovering themselves in the process. Our women set out on this developmental journey with a sense of power in their intuitive processes and a newfound energy and openness to novelty. (p. 77)

Liz found excitement and energy in the learning of the ideas presented in the science curriculum. She was eager to share in the journey of learning along with her students. Her acceptance of the learning *as* teaching gave her the power of owning and shaping the curriculum as her own.

The ideas of how teachers perceive reform efforts, the impact of researchers or other outsiders involved in the project, and how these affect the ways that teachers "own" or "know" the process of change all impact the ways that teaching and learning occur in classrooms. Teachers, like the women that Belenky et al. describe, find ways to create teaching and learning experiences in their classroom that they can understand. Creating the ownership is a personal process for the teachers. They draw from their perceptions about the context in which they work, their experiences, and their sense of control over events in their classroom, along with their views about teaching and learning to *know* the new curriculum and pedagogies.

NOTE

1. The aide is a certified teacher who works with the four sections of first grade because they have larger numbers in their classes—24 students—but the school board offered to hire an aide or hire another teacher. They opted for the aide as they did not know what space and materials there would be for another class and the option was presented only one week before school started. The aide seems to work very well with both the kids and the teachers and was hired the following year to take the place of a retiring first-grade teacher.

CHAPTER 6

A ROOM OF ONE'S OWN

Concrete and Conceptual Spaces

Not a flat, not an apartment in back. Not a man's house. Not a daddy's. A house all my own. With my porch and my pillow, my pretty purple petunias. My books and my stories. My two shoes waiting beside the bed. Nobody to shake a stick at. Nobody's garbage to pick up after.

   Only a house quiet as snow, a space for myself to go, clean as paper before the poem. (Cisneros, 1984, p. 108)

JENNIE'S STORY (PART 1): A ROOM OF ONE'S OWN

Jennie's classroom is her own. It is warm and inviting. The students' desks are arranged in five groups of four, and this cluster forms the focus of the classroom. It is evident that this is where the central activity of the class takes place. There are no chalkboards, and the teacher's desk is unassumingly placed at the back of the room. Children's work hangs on the walls—both individual projects and classroom ideas. There is a table in one corner that is piled with examples of leaves and other plant life that the children have brought in. Laminated projects from former third-grade students also sit on the back table as evidence of the family atmosphere and value for student work that Jennie holds in her classroom. Along another side of the room is a class set of plants developing under fluorescent grow lights and placed on a self-watering system. The Wiscon-

Teachers and the Reform of Elementary Science, 107–119
Copyright © 2004 by Information Age Publishing
All rights of reproduction in any form reserved.

sin Fast-Plants are just beginning to form flowers and several of the students look at them before they sit down in their seats. They have just returned from physical education. On this particular day, there are five adults in the room. There is a special education assistant, a grade-level teaching assistant, myself, the principal, who is evaluating Jennie's teaching, and Jennie. It does not seem crowded and the kids welcome the adults into their projects willingly, as does Jennie. She is comfortable in her room and in her teaching and makes all of us feel a part of the teaching and learning that occurs. Her warm and inviting classroom is a reflection of the teacher and teaching that has created this space.

From the moment that preservice teachers begin their formal education as education majors they speak about having their own classroom. I know this from listening to the elementary education students whom I teach and also because I once was one of these teachers waiting to create my own space for teaching. Preservice teachers watch and occupy the space of mentor teachers. They take all of the differing ideas that they see and make their own ideal for what their teaching will look like. They see more than the decor of these rooms. They see attitudes and ideas that they want to replicate and those that they want to disown. They crave the opportunity to design and implement their own ideas. A teacher's classroom is his or her own space. It is a space that is occupied not only physically but also mentally while engaging in the creative act of teaching and making decisions about the whats and the hows of the ways that the curriculum will be enacted. Many factors influence these decisions (colleagues, state, national, and local standards, administration, community, etc.), but it is the different ways that every teacher creates his or her own space for teaching that is interesting to me. Teachers create their own spaces for making changes in pedagogy and curriculum. The metaphor of a room of one's own, based on feminist writings on space, place, and relationships, describes this process.

Virginia Woolf wrote about creative process (and I believe teaching is a creative process) as a "room of one's own." As Woolf describes a room of one's own where women writers need to have space and freedom to create, teachers also need to have the freedom and space to think about teaching practices and make these their own. This is especially pertinent when teachers are confronted with pedagogical reforms. This approach to curricular and pedagogical change emphasizes the construction of understanding of reform efforts and is based on the belief that there is no single, effective method for teaching and learning as students and teachers differ in their preferences, desires, imaginations, attitudes, and interests. As the teachers "do" science activities, try activities out with their students and in their classroom settings, and reflect on these experiences, their knowledge of science and science teaching is expanded. In order to make this new knowledge a part of their understanding of teaching practice, each individual must create an understanding that meshes with their prior science teaching experiences. Like a blank paper before writing a poem (Cisneros, 1984), there is much possibility for ideas, but expectations, attitudes, emotions, imaginations, and desires play a part in how the poem is created.

In this chapter, I will further elaborate on this metaphor, using narratives to illustrate how teachers create spaces for understanding and implementing reform efforts in their own classrooms. This project has set aside spaces for teachers to make their own understandings of curricular and pedagogical changes in science teachings. I will tell stories of two teachers involved in the process, and describe part of their journey in making changes in their classrooms. By telling their stories, I hope to relate that when teachers make decisions about the creative process of teaching and are given space do this creating, they form their own understandings of curricular and pedagogical reforms.

TEACHERS AS SPACE MAKERS

When teachers are given spaces (both conceptually and concretely) to make their own sense and understanding of their emotions and attitudes about science and science teaching, they are given a powerful place.[1] It is the power to create understanding for themselves, making the new a part of their own knowledge and creating a way for new methods to become their own. When teachers work together to support one another in their learning efforts, in trying new ideas, and in talking about and reflecting on their ideas and practice, they gain a certain strength and self-confidence in the ways they work with each other, their students, and their ideas. In time, they develop a broader understanding of learning, teaching, and education, an increased knowledge of themselves as learners, and a more complex understanding of the nature of science. This seems to be important in their understandings and in developing a critical reflective way of approaching science teaching and learning.

ALICE'S STORY: CREATING A SPACE OF HER OWN

Alice has been teaching for more than 20 years. She is a second-grade teacher who did not actively participate in the science reform efforts during the project's first year. By not actively participating, I mean that she did not pilot any of the second-grade units and she was not a member of the district science committee. However, Alice did participate in grade-level planning meetings where teachers met to talk about, look at, and evaluate possible curriculum, topics, and materials. She became aware of the curricular and pedagogical changes to which the district had made a commitment. In the spring of 1999, Alice signed up to teach a group of students during the district's summer science camp. She "wanted to find out more about the new science program." Through teaching and by participating in activities designed for the teachers, Alice would also gain graduate credit as the first two weeks of the camp. Attached to the camp is a graduate class for the teachers where they are given an opportunity to learn about inquiry methods of learning by doing science themselves. Part of the requirement of the course was to keep a journal documenting these experiences. Alice wrote:

> I know the first day we met I wasn't sure what to do with the roly-poly and sow bugs. Those were things I would just as soon step on, but it only took a few minutes and I was noticing all kinds of things about them. Then we were asked to draw and write about what we saw. My first thought was I don't want to do this, but then it became fun and I learned in spite of myself.

Alice was one of the teachers who volunteered to share her writing with the teacher group. She had written a poem about the bugs.

> Mr. Bug, I have a question
> Are you a roly poly or a sow bug?
> Whenever we're asked we say
> See if you can make us curl into a ball
> and roll around on the ground.
> Mr. Bug, I have a question
> Are you an insect?
> Whenever we're asked we say
> Count our legs to see if we have more than six.
> Mr. Bug, I have a question
> Where is you habitat?
> Whenever we're asked we say
> Look under old wood, flower pots, or crocks
> Wherever it is damp or wet.

Alice told me that she had forgotten how much fun it was to observe and look at things. She was a teacher who taught from the science textbook, making it through the entire book every year. Again from her journal:

> In the past the class has read the chapters together in Science and answered the questions at the end in a 30 minute block of time. Next year I hope to arrange my schedule to have a larger block of time, do more hands-on science in groups of 2 or 4. We will do more chart work and journal writing. Also, I will be doing more linking of curriculum. I hope to work with the art teacher to learn some of the art techniques we might use during science activities. I want to make these changes because science camp has shown me that children respond to this kind of learning with eagerness and curiosity. Not only do they learn information, they also gain social skills and responsi-

bility. There are more opportunities for problem solving and thinking skills to develop. Participation in summer science camp has provided me the opportunity to participate and see this first hand.

I show these examples from Alice's journal because she has changed her view of teaching and learning science so radically and attributes the change to her firsthand experience and opportunity to try out the ideas herself. Alice found the "space" that allowed her to make the changes. She needed to see and experience inquiry science teaching and learning for herself before she could understand and envision the way that it would work in her own classroom. This experience gave her the confidence to try the changes she proposed in her summer journal, and her experience in her own classroom has encouraged her to continue.

I have visited Alice's classroom several times this year, and each time she has greeted me smiling warmly and eager to show me the projects on which the children are working. Her room is filled with books about the topic of study, and the walls outside her classroom are covered with artwork and writing related to the topic. Her students are sitting in groups of two. She told me last week that she is glad that the district has changed to this curriculum. "It is more interesting for me and the students. They really look forward to science time and the activities. They enjoy the learning."

At one point, the second-grade teachers met to talk about the curriculum, share their experiences with the units that they have been teaching, and talk about problems, concerns, and suggestions they have about the new science program. This was in the middle of the first school year that all of the second-grade teachers were teaching the new curriculum. They all had taught a unit on butterflies and Alice was eager to share her successful experience with "failure."

My caterpillars from the company was a terrible experience. They arrived late, they did everything that we were supposed to study over the weekend, so our lessons on observing the changes were pretty much nonlessons. So I had an idea. I quickly wrote a note home asking everyone to bring in a caterpillar that they found, being careful to note where they found it and what it was eating. I didn't know how many I would get. It was the end of the season, getting cold and all. I had so many different caterpillars! We learned so much—what they all ate, what kinds of different changes they all went through, and on and on. The kids just kept them on their desks and brought in what they ate. It really turned out great and all because of a mistake in the ordering! One of the kid's caterpillars came out of its chrysalis right in the middle of math—we just all stopped and gathered around his desk. He was like a proud father with his new butterfly!

Alice's excitement in her story was passed to the other teachers. She was the expert as they asked her question after question about how she structured the activity. How much time did she allow for the lessons? How did the kids do all day with containers of caterpillars on their desks? How did she make time for these extra activities in the curriculum? To answer these questions, she said fairly confidently, "I just don't worry about it too much. I figure we'll just keep studying until we're done." Alice, who said that she remembered how much fun it was to learn when she did the science activities herself, was seeing this excitement in her students. Because of her own experience, the doing of the science activities and the motivation that these activities provided for continued learning became the center of her science curriculum. She let that experience influence the way that her science teaching looked and the way that her classroom looked and felt as she taught and talked about science with her students.

Alice was "given" a space to work through her own perceptions of what science teaching and learning are. She had time in the science camp to try the new pedagogy and theories for herself and with students. There was a structured time to talk about this experience and an assignment to write about her experiences. Teachers supported one another as they team taught the summer classes. When Alice returned to school in the fall, this structured support continued as her building principal continued to support the science program, encouraging teachers to implement the program in their classrooms. I believe these given spaces did contribute to supporting the pedagogical and curricular changes that Alice implemented in her classroom. But what I believe to be more important is the space that Alice "created" for herself. She made changes in her own perceptions of what science teaching and learning are. She gave herself permission to understand what it meant to be interested and excited about learning and she began to implement these new perceptions into her teaching. Without the space that Alice created for herself, the imposed structures to facilitate change could make no difference. Alice, in her own space and in her own classroom, holds the power for the success or failure of school reform efforts. Structures designed to implement pedagogical and curricular changes need to acknowledge, facilitate, and celebrate the importance of that power.

DAVID'S STORY: CONVERSATION FOR
MAKING HIS OWN UNDERSTANDING

David was not an original member of the science committee. Because of his own interest in science teaching and curriculum changes that would affect him, his teaching, and his students, David became involved in the project from the very beginning. He did not participate in either of the summer science camps because of his commitments as a coach, but he did come to the first meeting of the district science committee in the fall of 1998. The meeting took place in one of the fifth-grade classrooms. We met there because this particular teacher used tables for student work places and it lent itself well for a meeting of about 15 adults. There were representatives from each grade level as well as Margery, Marilyn, the administrator in charge, and myself. This was the first time that I met any of the teachers. It was also an introduction to the structure and wording of the grant that would fund the process of changing their science curriculum. This exchange took place between David and other teachers at that meeting.

> **David:** So, there are only four unit topics to be covered the entire year? Do you see them lasting a full nine weeks each?
>
> **Jennie:** Well, there is so much material and the kids are loving it. I'm hoping that I can get it all done before I have to move on.
>
> **Gordon:** (the administrator in charge of curriculum for the district) That's the mentality that we have to get away from. Now it's time for Science. Now it's time for Social Studies. We need to start thinking of the learning as a whole.
>
> **David:** That's easy for you to say, but I switch with another teacher and am locked into a schedule. I suppose we could combine classes and I teach science every day for a half hour. Will there be enough to last a whole nine weeks?
>
> **Liz:** It's a different approach. Instead of a smattering of subjects, we are going in depth on a few.
>
> **David:** So it's like if you teach multiplication in third grade then you don't get it again until it comes up in high school? Once the subjects are taught they aren't covered again.
>
> **Liz:** But now we are teaching things that aren't appropriate for some grade levels. This scope and sequence looks at the grade levels and it isn't the only time a subject is taught.

The teachers who answered David had already been piloting some of the units in their classrooms or had been a part of the summer science camp where they had tried some of the teaching. David had had no experience with the new curriculum, but was concerned about the way that it would impact the way his classroom and the science curriculum he had been teaching worked. He wondered what it meant to go in-depth, to only study a few topics, and how this would impact his teaching and his students. The new program directly challenged the way that he perceived his success in teaching. In order for him to accept the change he would have to understand how a process-approach science curriculum fit into his understanding of teaching and learning.

As I got to know David, through visits to his room, through grade-level planning meetings, and through informal conversations, the reasons why David asked and continued to ask these questions became more clear to me, and perhaps to him as well. David really wanted to understand the underlying reasons for the curricular and pedagogical changes and he wanted these reasons to make sense to him. David took teaching seriously. He, like the other male teachers at the school, wore a tie every day. He was the only member of his immediate family and much of his extended family to go to college and to leave the small blue-collar town in which he grew up. Education was important to him. David lives in the community, his own children go and will go to school here, and his wife is also a trained teacher who works as a teacher assistant in the school. He volunteered to pilot the unit his grade level was piloting to "better understand the changes being made."

He wanted to make sure that his goals for teaching met the expectations of his community, the state, his administrators, and most importantly that they delivered what he believed to be good science teaching. He wanted to "know" that his students came away from his classroom ready to go to fourth grade, ready to pass the standardized tests, and ready to understand some basic science facts and concepts. David was not convinced that the new curriculum would meet these expectations. At one point he made a list of the topics covered on the tests to show me. "Think about it. If the tests are in early spring that means my class will have only covered two maybe three topics. That's not what the tests expect that we've covered." David did not feel that the four in-depth units taught by each grade level would give the students enough content coverage to perform well on the state and district tests.

As I stated in earlier chapters, David was worried about the test scores, accountability for knowledge, and concerned about the amount of content, vocabulary and time spent on each unit. David continued to ask questions and began to make adjustments in his teaching to fulfill his own need to fit the new curriculum into his own understanding of his role as science teacher. He added his own vocabulary lessons and tests to the units and found that he became more of a guide during science class investigations. He thought about parts of the changes that he did think were good for science teaching and learning in his classroom, "There is lots of hands-on. It allows students to explore. Students learn to record data and they learn how to interact in group work." David was not completely satisfied with the program and the changes made in the district science curriculum. He continued to have concerns that needed to be addressed if the new curriculum was going to play a role in his science classes.

David was also concerned about the bigger picture of the topics taught and the depth of the topics taught across the grade levels. Part of the reason for a change in curriculum and the discussion of the science curriculum, according to David, was a lack of communication between grade levels and within grade levels about what science was taught. Each teacher "did their own thing" and some topics were covered every year and others were never covered. David now sees this as not such an important issue. "If the focus is on the thinking skills and the processes, it really doesn't matter what the topics are." This was stated as part of a discussion of teachers being "territorial" about their science unit topics. Teachers are very protective of the spaces they create. David developed a wider view of this space as he worked to understand the impact of the new curriculum on the district as a whole. He asked the high school science teacher if he thought that the elementary curriculum would prepare the students for high school science classes. The high school teacher responded in a positive manner. For David, the answer became part of his own understanding of where his teaching fit into the district's science program. For him, the understanding of the program and its ability to meet the expectations of everyone David is required to please, including himself, is the search that David continues.

Virginia Woolf (1929/1957) gave women the advice to write for themselves: "[I]t is much more important to be oneself than anything else. Do not dream of influencing other people.... Think of things in themselves" (p. 111). Perhaps this is the advice that David should take. Teach for yourself; teach what and how feels right to you. This is the dilemma he faces (and with which many teachers struggle). How can you work for your community, with your colleagues and administration, and with your students and also teach for yourself? How can all of these ideas negotiate a space in teachers' classrooms?

JENNIE'S STORY (PART 2): A COMFORT ZONE

David and Alice were working to find a level of comfort with the changes. Like Liz and Sandy, who took ownership of the project right away, Jennie's philosophy and teaching style matched the ideas presented in the new science curriculum and hands-on pedagogy. She used the kits, but added in many of her own activities. The changes did not seem to concern her much; she was comfortable with the reforms. When I visited her classroom, she seemed generally enthusiastic about teaching and the science curriculum just became a part of that teaching. It was an easier transition because these were ideas that Jennie had already considered in her classroom. On the particular day that I described earlier in this chapter, a day on which Jennie was being evaluated by her principal, a teacher assistant was in the room to help with a special education student, and another teaching assistant was there to assist with science, the students were studying leaves. They had been on a nature walk earlier in the week to a park. In the park, the trees were labeled with their names and the students were required to pick up as many different kinds of leaves as they could find. Jennie and the two assistant teachers passed out the bags of leaves that the children collected and Jennie instructed the children on how to flatten the leaves in the magazines she had placed in the middle of their table groupings. The students would be using the leaves, not only to observe patterns, shapes, and morphology, but also to complete an art project where they would create a picture out of the leaves. Her example was a dog created from several leaves that she had pressed and glued on a large poster board. Jennie added this activity, which she did each fall with her class, to the unit on plant growth to expand the lessons to the kids' own environment. The kids took their time taking their leaves from their plastic grocery bags and placing them carefully between the pages of the magazines. When they were finished, they placed the magazines under piles of encyclopedias on top of the bookshelves around the perimeter of the classroom.

This activity may not seem unique to anyone who has taught elementary students. What stood out to me was the natural way in which Jennie used this art activity to relate concepts of leaf shape, leaf patterns, and leaf parts throughout the lesson. What could have easily been a chaotic situation, a nerve-racking situation with so many adult observers in the room was an active learning environment. As the kids were working, Jennie walked through the room questioning the kids about their leaves, asking them to notice colors, shapes, patterns, and parts of their individual leaves. The kids were actively working on their describing and classifying skills. They were also taking note of the parts of the leaves which was a direct correlation to their on-going plant study. The atmosphere was comfortable, the kids and the adults accomplished their learning and teaching goals. Jennie's room was a zone of comfort because she was comfortable in leading the learning—she was comfortable with the content, the process, and with facilitating her students' experiences.

QUESTIONING THE PROCESS

My role has been to support the classroom teachers in the design and implementation process. I did this by helping during science lessons in classrooms, listening to teachers talk about their experiences with the curriculum, and participating in planning meetings where teachers share with each other their experiences with teaching the new curriculum. In this role, I have seen the teachers try out new teaching practices and try to develop an understanding of them. They wanted to understand and feel that they were doing the right things, that their students were learning, and that they were teaching. In teaching in a more process-oriented approach, they had given up some of their control and the understanding that they had of teaching and learning. They were taking their new experiences with learning and creating a new understanding of their own place.

David and Alice are examples of teachers who began to make changes in their practice, reforming what teaching and learning look like in their classrooms. Their understandings were created very differently as they worked in their own ways to fit the new curriculum into their previous experiences and understanding of science teaching and learning. David needed to seek answers to his questions. He conversed with other teachers, administrators, and others to work toward an understanding of the benefits and pitfalls of the new curriculum. In this way, his research made him an "expert" on the process and he began to look at the big picture, defending the program as he worked to implement it in his classroom. Alice was convinced of the merits of the changes as she became excited about her own learning and her students' enthusiasm. Through the support of her principal and other teachers in her building, she felt her classroom was a safe place to experiment with the curriculum. She had permission to try the hands-on projects without worry of making mistakes. She felt the learning was in the experience. Jennie, was already comfortable with the ideas of the reform and could easily implement the efforts into her lessons and teaching. By looking at their stories, we see how these teachers created rooms of their own. They were given space and freedom to create the ways that the new curriculum would become a part of their own classroom teaching. Their classrooms became a reflection of the teachers and the teachers' own understanding of the reform efforts.

INDIVIDUAL SPACES

The stories from teachers I worked with on this project are examples of different ways that particular teachers have created spaces for making the science curriculum their own. They tried to answer questions about the process of reforming the science curriculum for themselves, but in very different ways. Alice worked towards her own understanding of her role in the process of changing science curriculum by doing the science herself and remembering how exciting learning can be. For David, it was not enough to see his students engaged in the process of learning. He wanted to justify and answer the questions about the curriculum and his role pragmatically. I have chosen these stories not only because they support my concept of individual spaces, but also because they show that these spaces are both concrete and conceptual. David's individual space is an intellectual space—a space where he works out the questions and concerns he has by thinking through the ideas. Alice's individual space is an emotional space where she is supported by her administration and the other teachers in her building to try out new pedagogies. Jennie's is a physical space that reflects ideas that support the reform efforts—the kids are working in groups, the room is filled with items supporting the science learning, and there is a general feeling of warmth. All of these conceptual and concrete spaces are personal reflections of the ways that teachers have created comfort zones for themselves. They are places where the teachers can make themselves comfortable with the reform efforts—intellectually, emotionally, and physically. The teachers reflect these spaces in the ways that they think about teaching and learning science and also in the changes that they have made in their doing of the teaching and learning of science.

The teachers also made these changes in their practice in ways that point out what is problematic in the metaphor. A room of one's own implies individualistic creation when teaching is anything but; it implies a powerful position when it is not, it implies that they have had the space and the time to think about their practice and apply this to their teaching. Woolf's metaphor in relation to women writers having a space void of the other responsibilities of women's (and men's) lives is unrealistic—we cannot be free of their other responsibilities such as mothering/fathering and societal and household tasks, nor would all of us want to be free of our responsibilities. We learn to balance and juggle these responsibilities, finding the space for them to overlap and influence one another. Women writers do not work in a vacuum where they concentrate only on writing. Women's lives are complicated. Women have had to put together a mosaic of activities and resolve conflicting demands on their time and attention (Bateson, 1989, p. 13). Bateson utilizes the metaphor of a crazy quilt to describe the way that women "compose" the experiences of their lives. The experiences/quilt may look "willy-nilly," but "the various pieces, wherever they come from, have to be trimmed and shaped and arranged how they fit together" (Bateson, 1989, p. 13). I saw the teachers make sense of curricular and pedagogical changes in a similar way. As I listened to their conversations during meetings, as they reflected on "doing" science, on their teaching, their lessons, and their classroom experiences, they wove their experiences, creating conversations that moved from one experience to another but in some way connected to the understandings that they were creating for themselves. As the teachers take in other's perspectives, new ideas, and new experiences, they work to find "the essence of themselves" (Lindbergh, 1955/1983). By creating structures (like meeting times and systems for collecting teaching materials) that gave them time to reflect on these experiences, share their ideas with their colleagues, and try these ideas in classrooms, the teachers formulated their own individual understandings of the curricular changes. These changes became part of their individual teaching and the room of their own.

A teacher's classroom is his or her own, but the space is created by a mosaic of influences. Teachers do not work in their own creative vacuum, but they do have influence over the patterns that emerge and over which themes are present in the foreground of their work. These stories show that teachers can and do make decisions about the creative process of teaching, work to make changes in their practice, and make decisions about the ways that these processes are enacted within their classrooms. The way that they implement the change process is a personal one, and because it is a personal process, school reform efforts largely depend on the teachers making these efforts a part of their own thinking, teaching, and learning. By giving teachers a space to understand their conceptions about science learning, teachers learn to articulate their own philosophy of education—what they think about the curricular and pedagogical reforms. As the teachers did the science themselves, reflected on this experience, and then tried the processes with children, they began to form their own understanding of the curricular and pedagogical changes.

NOTE

1. This implies that teachers will use the space that has been given to them to work toward change. For example, this "space" could be in the form of time for reflection and conversation or time and support for trying out new ideas. When I say "given," I mean provided by or supported by others who hold power (administration, colleagues, community).

CHAPTER 7

NEGOTIATING A SPACE TO TEACH SCIENCE

Stories of Community Conversations and Personal Process in a School Reform Effort

The reform effort that I have described took place over a two-year period. During this time the teachers worked to find the ways that the new science curriculum worked in their classrooms. They tried the science out on their own, with their students, and with each other—both actively and through conversations. Implementing the new science curriculum fit with many teachers' philosophies about how science should be taught and for others it was a big change. Negotiation and questioning of the pedagogy and the curriculum in their own classrooms became a part of the journey for all of the teachers. In my writing I have tried to explore that negotiation—the ways that teachers became involved in the process of changing curriculum and pedagogies and also the realities of implementing those changes in the classroom. How did teachers negotiate their place within changes in pedagogy and curriculum, and how is this negotiation enacted in the space of a teacher's own classroom?

At the end of this book, I do not claim to have the answers to these questions. Part of what I saw happen in Balmoral has led me to believe that no matter what kinds of reform efforts are tried in schools, it is ultimately the individual teacher who creates a place for that reform to take

Teachers and the Reform of Elementary Science, 121–136
Copyright © 2004 by Information Age Publishing
All rights of reproduction in any form reserved.

place in his/her classroom (or not take place). Change is a process. It takes investment of those involved, belief by those involved, and support for those involved. In my experiences with the Balmoral teachers, I saw how both internal and external factors played a role in how the science curriculum was taught by individual teachers. They all worked in a context that held high expectations, where test scores and content was perceived to be an important part of the learning and teaching. Yet, each teacher also brought values and philosophies of his/her own to the change process as well. These values and beliefs manifested themselves in relationships that they had with colleagues, the curriculum, and with their students. I also saw how the idea of ownership played a role in the ways that some teachers connected with the curriculum and also in ways that they created ownership for themselves. Teachers are ultimately in control of what happens in their classrooms in the very complex way that they are connected to the context in which they work. I hope that I have shown these complexities in the stories of personal change in the preceding chapters. What I think is one very important part of this book is the idea of the personal process of change. The individual stories of individual teachers show how change and reform impact teachers in a variety of professional and personal ways. The personal stories of teachers who are a part of a larger community and context enact the reforms in a variety of different ways in their individual classrooms. These stories have left me with questions that I believe people interested in school reform must consider as they work with or as teachers: (1) Teachers negotiate between larger contexts of their teaching and their own personal beliefs about teaching and learning. (2) Change is a continuous process and a natural part of teaching. (3) Teachers find ways to make imposed changes their own by making these continuous negotiations a part of their practice.

INDIVIDUALITY WITHIN THE CONTEXT OF COMMUNITY

Teaching is a personal/individual process that takes place within a larger community. This leads to a complex context for working and making decisions. In Chapter 2, I spent a great deal of space discussing the Balmoral teachers' work context. The standardized tests, the community expectations, as well as standards written by science reformers were all a part of the external context that these teachers worked within. These ideas were part of the larger community within which each teacher was a member. For David, who I described in Chapter 6 as he found a space for intellectualizing the reform efforts, the larger community of his school and his community played a large role in the ways that he viewed teaching and learning. The relationships with colleagues was also a part of that larger community. In Chapter 3, Gail viewed her relationship with Jan as an important part of how much she was willing to make changes. She was not willing to compromise her relationship and that complicated her own feelings about the reform efforts. These issues of balancing both the personal process of change with the larger context created dilemmas of how making changes in their classroom would compromise or challenge their beliefs about teaching and learning. Teachers have power and that power should be recognized. At times, that power may lead to some problems like Rob who crossed religious boundaries, but I think that this is a risk that we need to take. Decision making is a part of teaching and as professionals, teachers need to be trusted and encouraged to make decisions about what happens in their classrooms. I saw the teachers in Balmoral take that responsibility seriously as they reckoned with the changing curriculum and how it would impact teaching and learning in their classrooms, their schools, and their community.

> The variations of character and circumstance are infinite … and the moral being of narrative literature rests on the instinctive need of the culture as a whole to make bridge between precepts, rules and philosophies on one hand, and on character and character and circumstance on the other. Just as our lives are woven out of interactions between our emotional experiences and our intellectual interpretations and decisions, so the human world is a fabric of generally agreed upon rules interlaced by mitigating circumstances of identity or history. Stories, whether oral or written, whether narrated at an A.A. meeting or purchased in a bookstore or watched on television, make the necessary connections. Or culture is awash with stories. (Smiley, 1994, p. 48)

We look to individual stories to find a rationale "for acting in a moral or at least socially acceptable way" (Smiley, 1994, p. 48). Westheimer (1998, p. 8) agrees as he writes specifically about the idea of teacher community. "The idea of community is … elusive. There appears to be no central meaning." He also describes the tension that community brings to the idea of individuality, a tension he states that we have been trying to reconcile for more than two centuries between the ideals of individuality and community while understanding their complexities. I will not say that I have now an understanding of these complexities in the context of this small school district, but I do believe that those interested in school reform must pay attention to how teachers' ideals of individuality impact the reform efforts in the larger context of the school community, district, town, and larger society. The professional autonomy of a teacher is a negotiation of the boundary between an individual teacher's preferences and judgments and the needs of the community. There are complex relationships that play a role in the ways that reform efforts are enacted in classrooms.

I do not want to say that stories of teaching are narrative fiction, but they are narrative stories that hold some of the same tensions that Smiley describes. This quote from Smiley's (1994) essay, which is about creating character, also brings up the tensions that the teachers exhibited throughout this project: "How am I true to my own morals and act in a socially acceptable way? How can I find a way to teach that I am comfortable with, and also be a part of the larger school culture? How can I teach in a way that shows what I believe about teaching and learning and also connect to and serve the larger community in which I teach? Can I do what I need to do as well as what my students, parents, colleagues, administrators, reformers, and researchers expect?" These are questions that Bellah, Madsen, Sullivan, Swindler, and Tipton (1985) explored in their book *Habits of the Heart*. They contend that the language that we use to define ourselves as Americans bring us to a major moral dilemma. How can we resolve the conflict between our individualism and our need for community and commitment to one another? "The tension can be invigorating, helping to keep both individual and community vital and self-critical. But the tension is also anxious and sometimes leads to the potentially explosive conflicts between technical rationality and concrete commitments" (p. 154).

Technical rationality refers to solving a problem (of a community, a neighbor, something public) in an innovative (individualistic) way so as to keep the idea of both individual thought while also contributing to the community. Concrete commitments are ways that we measure ourselves against others. Both of these concepts can be directly related to the ways that the teachers expressed to me, both in conversation and in their teaching practices, how they worked through the changes in the science curriculum. Teachers felt a need to solve the problem (or make the curriculum work for themselves) in ways that would allow them to blend their own beliefs with what they felt was expected from them (making changes, keeping tests scores high, group work, covering content). The aspects that they could show to others became their concrete commitments. In other words, all of the teachers participated in the grade level planning meetings, sent their representatives to the science committee meetings, participated in the summer science camp course, et cetera, but they all implemented the curriculum and pedagogies in very personal and different ways. They worked to keep their own beliefs in the practice while also making a commitment to keeping themselves a part of their larger community.

Bell and Gilbert (1996) contend that teaching, "while supposedly an individual activity, is practiced in a public arena and is a social activity governed by rules and norms, however tightly or loosely defined" (p. 13). Many of the issues that I saw emerge from my study of the science project at Balmoral relate to this idea. The teachers seemed to see the teaching that they did in their classroom as a reflection of their schools and their community. They wanted to uphold the high test scores and the positive reputation that this district had maintained. They also saw their teaching as a reflection of themselves; they were proud of their district. I saw teachers find ways to balance the needs of the public arena of teaching with the personal beliefs they had about teaching and learning. For example, Gail enjoyed the activities she was doing as part of the new science curriculum, but she grappled with alienating herself from her teaching partner who did not share an equal amount of enthusiasm for the changes. She continues to look for the balance that will keep her a part of the larger social circle of teaching as well as find how she can continue to be enthused about her own classroom experiences. David grappled with a balance as well. He wanted to make sure that the larger context of the community and the state had a clear reflection of what the kids were learning. He found a balance by promoting an idea of mini-units, finding ways to incorporate more topics of study. He liked some of the ideas of the reforms, but he did not feel that they met his ideas of learning and teaching. He continues to negotiate the ideas of the reform efforts with the ideas of being accountable to his own community and students.

School districts are trying to foster a sense of community and professional ties among teachers by implementing changes in school organization.

> Site-based management, magnet programs, ... for example group students and teachers in more intimate, self-contained, autonomous clusters. Reformers hope to see teachers work together within these structures as colleagues and professionals. Ready to take responsibility for their own working environment as well as that of their students.... When reformers expect teachers to form professional communities, however, they imply that there exists an articulated and commonly understood notion of the type of community to which teachers aspire. (Westheimer, 1998, p. 10)

Westheimer continues to argue that there is not a consensus among teachers as to what professional communities are. Some teachers invite ideas of team-teaching, of collegial coaching, or observing and discussing with others their teaching practices, but many other teachers do not see these concepts as a part of their professional mission. "Current reforms that aim to build teacher professional communities do not adequately address these ambiguities, and may, in fact, encourage rather than reduce teacher isolation." In the Balmoral schools, the teachers were a part of what some might consider "professional communities." They were represented on science committees, had opportunities to make decisions about the content, supplies, materials and the general direction of the reforms. They had time to talk about their ideas and their experiences. Space was carved out for reflection, for sharing expertise, for trying out pedagogies, and for continued staff development with topics chosen by the teachers. Despite all of these efforts aimed at making teachers a part of this change process, the teachers still saw it as an imposed change. They did not see it as their own. This idea of owning the new curriculum and pedagogies became a process in its own. The teachers found ways, as I discussed in Chapter 5, to "own" parts of the changes.

IMPOSED CHANGES AND TEACHERS' OWN PRACTICE

Despite feeling that changes were imposed, teachers make the curriculum work for their needs in their own classrooms. When I say needs I mean finding ways to help the particular students and the particular group of students learn in the setting of their classroom. Teachers also have their own needs of interest, of acceptance, and of belief in curriculum and pedagogies. Teachers found ways to make the curriculum their own; they wanted to own what happened in their classrooms. Jennie (Chapter 6) who already agreed with many of the ideas of the new science curriculum easily found ownership in trying out the pedagogy and topics in her classroom. Mary, who I described in Chapter 3, continued to use textbooks and many aspects of the old curriculum as supplements to the new activity-based curriculum. Teachers found ways that they could own the curriculum through understanding as well. Alice, for example, tried out many of the lessons during the summer science camp and this emotional space of familiarity allowed her to "own" the lessons as she implemented them during the school year. For, David, as I described in Chapter 5 as we left one of the last science committee meetings, hearing that his concerns were being addressed made a difference in the way that he saw the program continuing. He began to believe that maybe there were ways to balance the reform efforts and the expectations of the state and achievement tests if the district made a commitment to teaching more topics through mini-units.

Every school has a curriculum, but everybody perceives the curriculum differently. "We teachers, particularly those of us in elementary school, teach who we are" (Ohanian, 1999, p. 9). Teachers take the curriculum, creating and acting on their curriculum knowledge, and interpret, shape, and adapt it to their particular contexts (Ben-Peretz, 1990). Bell and Gilbert (1996) say,

Learning and knowing (for example in a professional teaching situation) are not solely rational, logical activities, with affective dimensions. They involve the social renegotiation and reconstruction of what it means to be a teacher of science, including the construction of the teacher as a learner and someone who is changing his or her practice and beliefs throughout his or her career.... We adopt the position that the individual has some degree of responsibility and agency in the change process, while we also accept that an individual teacher has limited power to change the culture and socially constructed knowledge.

I would also add that reformers and researchers, administrators, colleagues also have limited power to change that culture and socially constructed knowledge. It really does come down to the individual teacher making choices and decisions about how to implement changes in his/her own classroom. Spaces can be carved to give teachers space to think, to reflect, to share, and to talk about the reform efforts; spaces aimed at helping teachers come to their own understandings of the changes.

Raymond (1986) writes about a concept translated from a Russian word, *zhiznerdostny*, which she calls "life-glad." She defines this concept as a process of looking for integrity with a purposeful energy in self-directed lives. I think that this concept Raymond uses in defining one aspect of female friendship could also be applied to teachers finding ways to make reform efforts part of their own understandings of teaching and learning. Teachers want to feel that the reforms are ideas that they are comfortable with (integrity to themselves and their beliefs) and ones that they can support and direct as they see fit in their own classrooms (purposeful energy and self-directed). Teachers need to make negotiations with these ideas as they consider new ideas as part of their teaching and learning context.

CHANGE AS A PROCESS, NOT A LOCATION

Change is a process that teachers view as part of their work. Teachers expect that they will adapt curriculum and make it work for the kids in their classes and for themselves. We need to change the ways that we look at reform and the ways that we present reform. It is often presented as a big change. For instance, in this project, although there was input and discussion from the teachers about the changes, the reform effort was presented as a change from one complete curriculum to another curriculum. We should be looking at reform as an on-going process. By making conversation and reflection a constant, teachers can more formally realize that reform efforts are part of this context of change and adapting curriculum. The conversation about gluing bees on the sticks to pollinate plants is an example of how teachers naturally share and reflect on what they do in their classrooms. Carving our spaces for conversation and also for doing gives teachers an opportunity to continue what they already do informally as they pass in the halls, share lunch in the workroom, or work together after school and during planning times. These spaces need to be recognized and celebrated as places where change is constantly occurring to work toward better teaching and learning. The ways that we go about changes and reform efforts is to present these big ideas and new curriculums. I believe that many reforms are ideas that teachers will make a part of how they teach if given an opportunity to explore and understand the curriculum and pedagogies for themselves. This needs to be a constant and on-going part of teachers' professional experience.

David told me, "I love change—I change my students seat around every week. I love our new reading series format[1]—but I still have doubts that changing completely to four science kits per year is the way our district should go." It was not change that David was opposed to, but the ideas presented in the change. In his mind, he felt the kids in his classes, and in the elementary science program as a whole, would not be exposed to enough science content. His views of teaching and learning science influenced the ways that he interpreted the reform efforts and they did not match what he thought best for the context in which he taught. Change was not something that David was ready to make immediately, it became a continuous process for him as he worked through accepting parts of the ideas as he intellectualized about how the changes related to his ideas of teaching and learning science.

Paris (1993) found that teachers saw change as a necessary part of their jobs, both to meet the needs of the learners in their classes, and to meet their own needs as teachers. Change "was required to make curriculum responsive to the very particular and ever-changing needs of their children, and necessary, as well, for their own satisfaction and professional growth as teachers" (p. 84). Change was seen as a constant process and constant part of the work of teachers.

Although changing the science curriculum from a text-oriented approach to a more inquiry and hands-on learning approach was the common goal of the reform efforts described in this project, the process of that change was what I tried to concentrate on. Change is not something that could be located to a specific event in this project, but something that occurred (and is continuous) throughout the project and in varying degrees and depths. Change is a process. Community "both shapes and is shaped by interaction and participation.... [T]he outcome is itself a process.... [C]urrent reforms rarely differentiate between organizational conditions and community-building processes" (Westheimer, 1998, p. 19). The structures I discussed in Chapter 3—site-based management, common planning time, collaboration, providing supplies for teaching—

can assist in carving out spaces for teachers to work together to find ways to change their practices. These concepts can promote ideas of collaboration, community and ideas of reform. But change is a process that, as Westheimer states, has to be shaped by interaction and participation in that process. If teachers decide to "buy into" the ideas set out in the curricular and pedagogical changes, and some may when given the opportunity to do so as a result of these structural supports, then they will participate in the process of change. Their participation depends so much more on other factors involved in creating the context in which teachers work. The issues in this particular case were not only issues related to the larger context of the school and community, described in Chapter 2, but also by those factors related to a personal process of deciding how the reforms are enacted in individual classrooms (relationships and ownership of the ideas).

As reform efforts are begun, ended, and continued in schools, we need to consider the way that we look at these projects. We should look at reform as a continuous process of change by building on the idea of ongoing professional development. By providing structural supports that carve out spaces for reflection, for communication, and for collaboration educators can take ownership of the personal process of change. Teachers need space where their ways of knowing and understanding the changes are celebrated and valued as part of the process.

LAURA'S STORY: A PROCESS OF CHANGE

Laura is a fifth grade teacher. I want to tell her story because she took her time with implementing the new science curriculum. She was a member of the original science committee, but really only began to make changes in her classroom during the second year of the project. Her story brings up several aspects of the changes the Balmoral teachers worked through, but it particularly highlights that change is a continuous enduring personal process. Laura is evolving in her use of the science tubs. The change to this curriculum and pedagogy is a process and it is a process that is continuing for her. The pedagogies, in her words, "fit with the direction her class was going," but she was having trouble finding ways to fit it all in. Laura implemented part of one unit the first year of the project and parts of another unit the second year of the project.

Her teaching situation is unique because she works in one large classroom with another teacher. They have two full fifth grade classes in their room together and team-teach. They work together but divide the responsibilities of planning and teaching. Laura is primarily responsible for the planning and teaching of science, but this does not mean that her partner is not involved in that subject. They constantly bounce ideas off of each other and work to integrate subject matter. Their teaching arrangement came from their suggestion to their administration. Both teachers were working on a graduate degree and they decided to do their final project on the concept of team-teaching. They used their own classroom as a model and as a place to test the ideas that they were reading about. The result is a partnership that has gone on for several years and in the words of one of the teachers, "A situation that I would like to keep until I retire."

Both teachers participated in the summer science camp during the last year of the project. They chose to work not with each other, but to work with others as their teaching partners. Laura worked with her husband who is a middle school teacher in the Balmoral district and her teaching partner worked with another fifth grade teacher. Laura's partnership with her husband was interesting because I think it highlights some of the ways that a teaching relationship where the parties sharing a philosophy can work to make changes in curriculum and pedagogy. I also think that their partnership allowed them to take teaching risks they might not have taken without a trusting and supportive partner (not that Laura did not have this support from the other fifth grade teachers). They were also able to continue their conversations about teaching outside of the classroom. The unit that Laura and Tim decided to teach was a two-week inquiry of spiders. In their classroom they structured the unit in a way that the inquiry was very child-guided and the study became a quest to answer questions that the kids had about spiders. This was a teaching risk because neither teacher had done such an inquiry before. The unit was structured in that Laura and Tim had specific goals in mind for their students and also had activities planned that would foster inquiry and observation as the students investigated spiders.

Many of the journal entries by Laura and Tim spoke of the other individual—how they both felt about a particular lesson or activity they had tried, or about the planning they were doing.

> Tim and I chose the unit on spiders because many people have a fear of spiders and don't realize all the good things they do for us. We are going to get more acquainted with spiders and look at how they behave in their natural environment and in their captured environment. When they are done, we want them to be able to look at organisms in nature using a scientist's process and perspective.... Tim and I both felt that we need to accumulate all their questions and make a class poster of them. We want the kids to tap into spider information that they have in their head, and then start building on that information.

Tim's ideas for their study read very similarly. They share a philosophy about learning that helps them in supporting each other in their teaching.

> We chose to do a unit on spiders because they are not only an interesting topic, but they also play an important role in our world. Another important goal was that we wanted the students to participate in activities that they could go and do on their own when they were not in class. We wanted them to learn the process of asking a question, hypothesizing about it, and gathering results. We hope that by the end of the two weeks that the students will on their own go out and investigate the world around them.

The emotional support they could offer each other helped Tim to show their students some of his own inquiry. Tim did not consider himself a "creative teacher" and was reluctant to read to the teacher group when we shared our nature journals. Laura commented on the positive reaction that the kids had to Tim reading his poems to the class: "Tim shared his poem that he did on the Sweet Gum Tree. The kids seem to like that Tim is sharing some of his work with the class." From a list of describing words Tim compiled about a sweet gum tree (strong, tall, straight, tinged with red, brown, rough, wind can rock, grooves), Tim wrote the following poem:

> The tree stands tall
> And has a strong look.
> The bark is full of grooves
> And has a rough surface.
> Looking at the straight trunk
> The brown color shows a tinge of red.
> Even though the bark is hard
> The wind can rock the tree.

What happened in their summer classroom also shows the ways that these two teachers found their own experiences with learning science to impact the kinds of teaching and learning that they wanted to try in their classrooms.

> The experiences out at Marilyn's house have been helpful in how we choose to implement our activities. We are having the students do more hands-on activities.... We are also going to include the live specimens in their classification group. I realize from working at Marilyn's that working with real things seems to put science content into perspective.

After trying it in the classroom, they thought about ways that the projects they were working on might fit into their teaching and learning during the school year. Laura described how she saw how working in groups for a particular writing assignment was beneficial:

> I was a little leery about using this writing assignment because I struggled with it when I did my own nature journal. After doing this with our small group, I most definitely can see that this is a writing assignment that must be done in groups. I was impressed with all the different directions people took. The ideas were flowing great with the whole group. One person would say something and it got another person really thinking about it. It was contagious, and the legends were one of their favorite writing assignments. Many of the students got up and shared their creations.

Laura took her own experience integrating writing with science inquiry and changed the activity to better fit the needs of her students. In the time that she and Tim took to plan the science course, Laura reflected and adapted what she had found to be a difficult writing assignment. She was willing to carve out time during the class to try the assignment again and found that her changes gave her students a much more positive experience with the legend writing. This was a process—doing, reflecting, adapting, and teaching—a process that gave Laura confidence in changes she might try in her classroom during the school year.

They both found ways that the things that they were doing fit in with what they already believed about science teaching and learning. Laura wrote in her journal about two of the writing assignments their summer class completed:

> I like both the "I Wonder" poem and "The List" poem[2] because they are really things that I have done before, but I didn't have the students take it the one step further and put it in a more literature way. I see myself using both of these next year. I think that overall the kids' response to them was good.... I was really surprised that half of the class chose to share their poems out loud in front of the rest of the class. They were truly proud of them.

She also wrote:

> The Spider Study journals I think are one of the biggest things I am taking away from this class. I will use this type of study journal definitely with my cricket unit and I am sure I will implement other ideas from this open expression style. I love to see kids create with their own style. I feel that my classroom was moving in this direction last year.... [With some ongoing projects] the kids were in charge from the beginning to the end. They were given an assignment with many ways they could reach a final product. The nature journals helped me focus on how I might use these ideas in science.

Laura found some of the new pedagogical suggestions fit in with the ways that she was setting up the teaching and learning in her classroom. In Tim's case, the ideas he was trying highlighted a dilemma of trying out some more creative projects in his classes:

> I see myself looking and trying to implement ways in which kids can express themselves in their own creative ways. Time is a problem in my classes. I find I am crunched to get my whole curriculum in the time provided. This is why I haven't always opted to do writing and extra projects. However, it is a very valuable learning experience for the kids in doing projects and creative expression. I battle with the time problems and getting my whole curriculum in. It has been helpful to see some of these things implemented in the classroom; I realize that some of these activities don't really take that long and could be done.

His dilemma is similar to the voices of other teachers about not having enough time to do integrated, in-depth studies. How do teachers balance those kinds of projects with amount of content the feel they must cover?

From looking at Laura's experience, not just in the summer science camp, but her experience with the science program as a whole, the idea that change is something that happens over time and not something that can be located to a specific point is also highlighted. It took all of the experiences that Laura had with the new curriculum and her own experiences with teaching to bring together what will happen in her classroom in the fall as she continues to implement this science curriculum. Laura shared much of the philosophy of the science curriculum and had already been doing some of the science process skills combined with the old curriculum. Those experiences combined with her own exposure to the new curriculum and experiences with trying out those experiences herself and with children, are parts of the process that is change. Laura's curricular changes are not a linear process, but a process that combines and reacts, and reformulates all of the previous and on-going experiences to continue the process. This is an excerpt from Laura's final summer science journal that I think highlights many of the kinds of things that I saw the teachers work through at Balmoral:

> We are moving in the right direction with teaching science through processing activities; I am still evolving with the science tubs, but I feel I'm moving in a positive and productive direction. I had already started implementing more labs in connection with the science areas I taught. I saw the active learning that the students were involved in when we were doing lab work. The tubs have helped narrow down the topic areas that we cover in our science curriculum. Before, we covered such a wide range of areas, and you felt obligated to expose the children to as much as possible. Through the tubs, we can still expose the children to a lot, but it is focused more on one area.

We are studying things beyond the surface, and really getting to the core of why it is there, what makes it work, and how it is connected to us. This is a valuable learning process.

In this short journal entry, Laura brings up several aspects of the changes the Balmoral teachers worked through. She talks about content and process of science teaching—depth versus breadth. She talks about how the new curriculum fits in with her own ideas of what science teaching and learning are. And, she brings up an important idea in her first sentence: She is evolving in her use of the science tubs. The change to this curriculum and pedagogy is a process. It is a process that is continuing for her as she finds ways to balance her own beliefs about teaching and learning with the expectations of her teaching situation.

LEARNING COMMUNITIES AND
PERSONAL REFORM EXPERIENCE

I did not begin this project thinking that I would write about the ways that the context in which teachers work defines the ways that teaching reforms are enacted in classrooms. I began this project thinking that I would write about the ways that teachers worked together, were empowered and found excitement in creating a new science program for their school. That was a naïve view of the ways that change occurs in a school system. I was a teacher who had worked in schools where I had a lot of freedom to create curriculum and found that the relationships that I shared with other teachers fostered that creativity and power that we felt over our work. I know that there were other teachers in the schools that I worked in who were wonderful teachers, but did not necessarily embrace reform efforts. I did not think about all of the factors involved and the reasons why they might not feel that there was a need to change. I just always assumed that they were set in their ways. I think that this is a common view among many people who are stakeholders in our educational system: school boards, administrators, teachers, university researchers, community members, and parents. We do not think about the complex context that schools are—the place that they hold in our communities, the relationships between and among faculties, the culture of testing and standards that enters the classroom. Teachers find ways to arrange these ideas in their own space of their own classroom as they act on the ideas of curricular and pedagogical reform.

In an article that was written 25 years ago, Schwab (1976) discusses the idea of learning communities. He defines community as something that can be learned, that it is "a body of propensities toward action and feeling" (p. 235). These propensities can be learned and developed in social circumstances, which I believe that teaching is. He also states that learning is created by shared experiences, experiences that are given meaning by interacting with others through support, by imitation, and with collaboration. The *process* is one that must be rewarding for the participants. Schwab also argues that individuality in not something that is against the ideas of community, but individuality exists because of community.

> Identity, in brief, is not discovered by introspection but created through involvement with others—involvement in problems, involvement with the elements of culture. Individuality takes from only in continuous interplay with the persons and situations in which it comes to be. (Schwab, 1976, p. 239)

The Balmoral teachers used this "continuous interplay" with their colleagues, with their perceptions of what the state expected, with their community, with their teaching experiences as they personally negotiated the changes in their science program.

Schwab plays with the words learning and community to talk about these ideas: *learning* communities and learning *communities*. Both of these ideas play into each other and form one whole idea.

> The propensities that constitute community are learned only as we undergo with others the processes through which we learn other things. Meanwhile, the support, communication, and example that make it possible to learn these things become accessible and acceptable to us only as our propensities toward communities develop. (p. 235)

Without working with one another, we lessen the opportunities to continue learning from one another. And, without learning from one another, we lessen the opportunities to see the need for working with one another. Again, this is the tension that Bellah et al. (1985) explored in their study. How do Americans balance their need for being individualistic with the need to be part of a larger and bigger community? How can the ideas of being true to your own beliefs work within a context of tradition and commitment to your community? In the case of the teachers in Balmoral, I found each of them trying to find that balance in very different ways. They found ways that they could be true to the ideas of learning and teaching that they were comfortable with, but they also found that experience of change challenged and upset those existing ideas. Because the context of their work (relationships, community, tests) was an important factor to most of the teachers, the ideas of change brought them into a negotiation to find a new balance for understanding. These negotiations became personal processes that each teacher went through. The impact of these negotiations was evident in different ways that the curricular and pedagogical changes were implemented in each individual classroom.

The issues explored in this book do not attempt to provide an answer for how to implement changes in schools, but to challenge those involved in reform efforts to think about the context that teachers work in and to carve out spaces for teachers to find understanding, ownership, and community for reflecting on their practice. We need to remember that change is a personal process that is complex: it occurs in the context of teachers' classrooms, their communities, and in their relationships with the curriculum, the pedagogies, colleagues, and students. Change is not purely an outcome. It is a state of flux—a negotiation between things that equal in the insistence of their demands, and in some ways are fundamentally irreconcilable.

NOTES

1. The Balmoral elementary schools were also piloting and then implementing a new reading series during the same time frame as this science project.
2. The "I Wonder" poem uses student questions about the inquiry topic as a basis for the poetry. "The List" poem uses a list of information or of descriptive words from observation as the basis for the poetry.

REFERENCES

American Association for the Advancement of Science. (1989). *Science for all Americans*. Washington, DC: AAAS Press.

American Association for the Advancement of Science. (1993). *Benchmarks for scientific literacy*. New York: Oxford University Press.

Ball, D. L., & Cohen, D. K. (1996). Reform by the book: What is—or might be—the role of curriculum materials in teacher learning and instructional reform? *Educational Researcher, 25*(9), 6-8.

Balmoral Community School District. (1998). *School report card*. Balmoral, IL: Author.

Bateson, M. C. (1989). *Composing a life*. New York: Atlantic Monthly Press.

Belenky, M. F., Clinchy, B. M., Goldberger, N. R., & Tarule, J. M. (1986). *Women's ways of knowing: The development of self, voice, and mind*. New York: Basic Books.

Bell, B., & Gilbert, J. (1996). *Teacher development: A model from science education*. London, England: Falmer.

Bellah, R. N., Madsen, R., Sullivan, W. M., Swindler, A., & Tipton, S. T. (1985). *Habits of the heart: Individualism and commitment in American life*. New York: Harper & Row.

Ben-Peretz, M. (1990). *The teacher-curriculum encounter: Freeing teachers from the tyranny of texts*. Albany: State University of New York Press.

Ben-Peretz, M., & Silberstein, M. (1985, March-April). *Is this curriculum fit for teachers?* Paper presented at the annual meeting of the American Educational Research Association, Chicago, IL.

Chancer, J., & Rester-Zodrow, G. (1997). *Moon journals: Writing, art, and inquiry through focused nature study*. Portsmouth, NH: Heinemann.

Cisneros, S. (1984). *The house on Mango street*. New York: Vintage Books.

Clandinin, D. J. (1985). Personal practical knowledge: A study of teachers' classroom images. *Curriculum Inquiry, 15*, 361-385.

Clandinin, D. J., & Connelly, F. M. (1992). Teacher as curriculum maker. In P. W. Jackson (Ed.), *Handbook of research on curriculum* (pp. 363-401). New York: MacMillan.

Clift, R. T., Veal, M. L., Holland, P., Johnson, M., & McCarthy, J. (1995). *Collaborative leadership and shared decision making: Teachers, principals, and university professors.* New York: Teachers College Press.

Connelly, F. M., & Clandinin, D. J. (1988). *Teachers as curriculum planners: Narratives of experience.* New York: Teachers College Press.

Connelly, F. M., & Clandinin, D. J. (1995). Teachers' professional knowledge landscapes: Secret, sacred, and cover stories. In *Teachers' professional knowledge landscapes* (pp. 3-15). New York: Teachers College Press.

Connelly, F. M., & Elbaz, F. (1980). Conceptual bases for curriculum thought: A teacher's perspective. In A. W. Foshay (Ed.), *Considered action for curriculum improvement.* Alexandria, VA: Association for Supervision and Curriculum Development.

Deal, T. E., & Peterson, K. D. (1991). *The principal's role in shaping school culture.* Washington, DC: U. S. Government Printing Office.

Dewey, J. (1944). *Democracy and education.* New York: Collier Books. (Original work published in 1916)

Duckworth, E. (1987). *The having of wonderful ideas and other essays on teaching and learning.* New York: Teachers College, Columbia University.

Duckworth, E. (Ed.). (1990). Opening the world. In *Science education: A minds-on approach for the elementary years* (pp. 21-59). Hillsdale, NJ: Erlbaum Associates.

Easley, J. (1990). Stressing dialogic skill. In E. Duckworth (Ed.), *Science education: A minds-on approach for the elementary years* (pp. 61-95). Hillsdale, NJ: Erlbaum Associates.

Eisner, E. W. (1991). *The enlightened eye: Qualitative inquiry and the enhancement of educational practice.* New York: Macmillan.

Elbaz, F. (1981). The teacher's "practical knowledge": Report of a case study. *Curriculum Inquiry, 11,* 43-71.

Elbaz, F. (1983). *Teacher thinking: A study of practical knowledge.* London, England: Croom Helm.

Elbaz, F. (1991). Research on teacher's knowledge: The evolution of a discourse. *Journal of Curriculum Studies, 23,* 1-19.

Feinberg, W. (1998). Rejoinder: Meaning, pedagogy, and curriculum development: Feinberg answers Hirsch. *Educational Researcher, 27*(7), 30-36.

Fullan, M., & Hargreaves, A. (1996). *What's worth fighting for in your school.* New York: Teachers College, Columbia University.

Geertz, C. (1973). *The interpretation of cultures.* New York: Basic Books.

Grumet, M. R. (1987). The politics of personal knowledge. *Curriculum Inquiry, 17,* 319-329.

Grumet, M. R. (1988). *Bitter milk: Women and teaching.* Amherst: The University of Massachusetts Press.

Hawkins, D. (1974). Messing around with science. In *The informed vision: Essays on learning and human nature.* New York: Agathon Press.

Hirsch, E. D. (Ed.). (1992). *What your third grader needs to know: Fundamentals of a good third-grade education.* New York: Doubleday.

Hirsch, E. D., Jr. (1998). Response to Professor Feinberg. *Educational Researcher,* 27(2), 38-39.

Hollingsworth, S. (1994). *Teacher research and urban literacy education.* New York: Teacher's College Press.

Illinois State Board of Education. (1999a). *Illinois Learning Standards for Science.* Springfield, IL: Author.

Illinois State Board of Education. (1999b). *Programs for scientific literacy: Staff development projects.* Springfield, IL: Author.

Illinois State Board of Education. (2000a). *Programs for scientific literacy: Staff development projects.* Springfield, IL: Author.

Illinois State Board of Education. (2000b). *Sample test items of Illinois learning standards for science: Grades 4 and 7.* Springfield, IL: Author.

Kacich, T. (2000, June 25). Balmoral's windfall equals growth but some headaches. *The News Gazette,* p. B3.

Kantrowitz, B. (1999, September 6). Tests are an easy way out. *Newsweek,* 50-51.

Koch, J. (1999). *Science stories: Teachers and children as science learners.* Boston, MA: Houghton Mifflin.

Kliebard, H. M. (1997). The rise of scientific curriculum making and its aftermath. In D. J. Flinders. & S. J. Thorton (Eds.) *The curriculum studies reader* (pp. 31-40). New York Routledge. (Original work published 1975)

Lawrence-Lightfoot, S. & Davis, J. H. (1997). *The art and science of portraiture.* San Francisco, CA: Jossey-Bass.

Lincoln, Y., & Guba, E. (1985). *Naturalistic inquiry.* Newbury Park, CA: Sage.

Lindbergh, A. M. (1983). *Gift from the sea.* New York: Vintage Books. (Original work published 1955)

Liston, D. P., & Zeichner, K. M. (1996). *Culture and teaching.* Mahwah, NJ: Lawrence Erlbaum Associates.

McGinn, D. (1999, September 6). The big score. *Newsweek,* 47-51.

Meier, D. (2000). *Will standards save public education?* Boston, MA: Beacon Press.

National Commission on Excellence in Education. (1983). *A nation at risk: The imperative for educational reform.* Washington, DC: U. S. Department of Education.

National Research Council. (1996). *National science education standards.* Washington, DC: National Academy Press.

Noddings, N. (1992). *The challenge to care in schools: An alternative approach to education.* New York: Teachers College Press.

Ohanian, S. (1999). *One size fits few: The folly of educational standards.* Portsmouth, NH: Heinemann.

Paris, C. L. (1993). *Teacher agency and curriculum making in classrooms.* New York: Teachers College Press.

Quindlen, A. (1988). *Living out loud.* New York: Ivy Books.

Raymond, J. G. (1986). *A passion for friends: Toward a philosophy of female affection.* Boston, MA: Beacon Press.

Richardson, L. (1990). *Writing strategies: Reaching diverse audiences.* Newbury Park, CA: Sage.

Ryckman, L. L. (2000, September 24). Making the grade. *Denver Rocky Mountain News,* pp. 5A, 55A-59A.

Sarason, S. B. (1971). *The culture of the school and the problem of change.* Boston, MA: Allyn & Bacon.

Sarason, S. B. (1990). *The predictable failure of educational reform: Can we change course before it's too late?* San Fransisco, CA: Jossey-Bass.

Sarason, S. B. (1996). *Revisiting "the culture of the school and the problem of change".* New York: Teachers College Press.

Schmoker, M. (1996). *Results: The key to continuous school improvement.* Alexandria, VA: Association for Supervision and Curriculum Development.

Schwab, J. J. (1976). Education and the state: Learning community. In *Great ideas today* (pp. 234-271). Chicago, IL: Encyclopedia Britannica.

Schwille, J., Porter, A., Floden, R., Freeman, D., Knappen, L., Kuhs, T., & Schmidt, W. (1983). Teachers as policy brokers in the content of elementary school mathematics. In L. Schulman & G. Sykes (Eds.), *Handbook of teaching and policy* (pp. 370-391). New York: Longman.

Sergiovanni, T. J., & Starratt, R. J. (1993). *Supervision: A redefinition.* New York: McGraw-Hill.

Seuss, D., & Prelutsky, J. (1998). *Hooray for diffendoofer day!* New York: Alfred A. Knopf.

Skrabanek, D. W. (Ed.). (1998). *Parents' guide to standards.* Austin, TX: Steck-Vaugn.

Smiley, J. (1994). Can writers have friends? In M. Pearlman (Ed.), *Between friends: Writing women celebrate friendship* (pp. 44-55). Boston, MA: Houghton Mifflin.

Spillane, J. P. (1999). External reform initiatives and teacher' efforts to reconstruct their practice. *Journal of Curriculum Studies, 31*(2), 143-175.

Stake, R. (1995). *The art of case study research.* Thousand Oaks, CA: Sage.

Stanford Achievement Test. (1996). *Directions for administering: Complete/basic battery multiple choice* (9th ed.). San Antonio, TX: Harcourt Brace.

West, L. (1966). *A heritage reborn.* Piatt County, IL: Tour Illinois.

Westheimer, J. (1998). *Among school teachers: Community, autonomy and ideology in teachers' work.* New York: Teachers College Press.

Wolcott, H. (1994). *Transforming qualitative data: Description, analysis, and interpretation.* Thousand Oaks, CA: Sage.

Woolf, V. (1957). *A room of one's own.* San Diego, CA: Harcourt Brace Javanovich. (Original work published 1929)

INDEX

American Association for the Advancement of Science, 39

Assessment (see also Tests/testing), 38–39

Bateson, M., 18, 24, 95, 118

Belenky, M., 105–106

Bell, B., 124, 126

Bellah, R., 124, 135

Ben-Peretz, M., 7, 8, 126

Care, in education, 56; comfort, 63

Classroom environments, 57, 65, 116; as personal space, 3, 108

Clift, R, 53, 54, 92, 93

Change (see also Reform) 5, 9–10, 25, 122; as a continuous process 127–128, 129, 133, 136; as a personal process, 51, 68, 84, 86, 106, 119, 122, 134, 135; culture of, 37; in curriculum, 5, 33, 38, 41, 43, 108; in pedagogy, 3, 5, 6, 38, 41, 43, 108; in schools, 9,18, 51; process of vs. products of, 92, 101, 135

Cisneros, S., 107, 109

Community, and conversation, 16; and individuals, 122, 124, 135; in learning communities 134; in professional communities 125; in teacher communities, 122

Conversation, 12, 15, 16, 20–21, 45, 60, 61, 63, 77, 86, 118, 130; as method of inquiry, 12–13, 15;

collaborative conversation, 15, 16, 17, 20–21, 80, 90, 91, 128

Collaboration 53, 59, 61, 130; between university and public school, 53, 89; as protection, 54; feminist view of, 92; ownership and, 89, 97; roles within, 92, 94; "traditional" view of, 92; time for, 54, 60

Connelly, F.M., 7, 17

Curriculum 4, 5, 6, 33, 34, 40, 85; old curriculum vs. new curriculum, 34, 97,104, 115, 128; imposed curriculum, 8; science curriculum, 33, 37, 92

Culture, 35, 36, 122; culture of testing 37, 38; culture of change, 37

Clandinin,D. J., 7, 17

Dewey, J., 16, 39

Direct instruction, 48

Doing science, 58, 66, 85, 108, 112

Duckworth, E., 38, 39

Elbaz, F., 6, 7

Fullan, M., 9, 86

Grumet, M., 17, 94

Hargreaves, A., 9, 86

Hollingsworth, S., 15, 19, 80, 90

Illinois Standards Achievement Tests (ISAT), 2, 32, 42, 59, 63

Illinois State Board of Education (ISBE), 39, 43, 44, 46; Science and Literacy Grant, 11, 43, 44

Influences on teaching, 3; negotiation of influences, 3, 67, 69, 134; external demands, 3, 67, 108

Integrating curriculum, 82, 83, 85, 103, 110, 133

Inquiry, 2, 54, 65, 81, 90

Inquiry-based science curriculum 3, 11, 16, 19, 33, 38, 41, 44, 45, 46, 47, 75, 92, 93

Learning, as transaction, 34; as transmission, 34

Learning standards, 29, 35, 36, 39, 43, 47

Materials for teaching, 46, 71–76

A Nation at Risk, 37

Narrative, 14, 1617, 18, 19, 24, 122, 124; narrative inquiry, 17, 24, 94

Nature study, 81, 110, 131–132

Ohanian, S., 37, 126

Paris, C., 100, 128

Personal beliefs about teaching (see also teacher beliefs), 3, 5, 8, 23

Portraiture, 24–25

Process-oriented teaching and learning, 11, 33, 46, 47, 65, 76–77, 117

Quinlan, A., 61, 86

Raymond, J., 56, 127

Reflection, 55, 86, 108

Reform (see also Change), 3, 5,10, 13, 14, 18, 29, 37, 40, 47, 92; as a personal process, 75; constructing, 105, 117, 119; ownership of, 89, 100, 122, 126; school reform, 5, 9, 10, 51; through learning 105; through understanding, 102, 114; teacher role in, 5, 13, 86, 122;

Relationships, 3, 4, 51, 53, 54, 59–60, 67, 93, 129; impact on reform, 52, 122; friendship, 52, 56, 61, 93, 127; value of relationship, 54, 55; power of, 55; tension within, 66, 68; thoughtfulness in, 56; with learning, 58; with children, 64; with curriculum, 64, 66

Researcher, as artist, 23; as learner, 19; as listener, 19, 21, 23; as validator, 19, 22;

Richardson, L., 16, 17, 23, 94

Safe spaces, 84, 117

Science process skills, 2, 54, 56, 58, 66–67, 103, 105, 110

Science journals, 58, 68–69, 81–82

Science and religion, 59

Smiley, J., 123, 124

Space, 60, 75, 86, 127, 129, 136; emotional, 118; individual, 84, 112, 117; intellectual, 118; physical, 118; for collaboration, 68; for exchanging ideas, 55; for reflection, 55, 86, 109, 117; for questions, 55, 63, 112, 113

Spaces, safe, 84, 117

Staff development, 45–46

Standards, 29, 35, 36, 39, 43, 47

Standards-based movement, 37

Summer Science Camp, 12, 45, 48, 65, 68, 75, 76, 81, 95, 110, 130

Support, 52, 74; conceptual, 74, 112; structural, 44, 51, 74, 85, 112, 125

Teaching, as a creative process, 108; as learning, 64, 83, 105; excitement in, 63, 86, 111, 115; vulnerability in, 63, 84

Teacher beliefs, 36, 57–59, 103, 104, 114, 127, 128, 134

Teacher decisions, 3, 54, 60, 84, 100, 115, 119, 122

Teacher emotions, 109, 118, 131
Teacher needs, 57, 85, 114, 126
Teacher voice, 92, 94, 101
Teaching materials, 46, 71–76
Teaching, process-oriented, 11, 33, 46, 47, 65, 76–77, 117
Technical rationality, 124
Testing/tests, achievement tests, 27, 28, 29, 39, 40, 41, 42, 47; culture of, 37, 38; standardized tests, 36, 38, 43; *Stanford Achievement Test*, 41, 42; state tests [Illinois Standards Achievement Tests (ISAT)], 2, 32, 42, 59, 63
Textbook-based science curriculum, 3, 19, 35
Transactional way of learning, 34
Transmission way of learning, 34

Westheimer, J, 122, 125, 129
Women's ways of knowing, 105
Woolf, V., 108, 115
Writing activities,   poems, 58, 110, 131, 132

Printed in the United States
20675LVS00003BC/1-3